# H2H Defence.co.uk

Modern Self Defence & Conflict Management

CW00591543

# R.A.I.D.

## Rapid Action Initiated Defence

Copyright © 2013 Tremaine Kent

The moral right of the author has been asserted.

Apart from any fair dealing for the purposes of research or private study,
or criticism or review, as permitted under the Copyright, Designs and Patents
Act 1988, this publication may only be reproduced, stored or transmitted, in
any form or by any means, with the prior permission in writing of the
publishers, or in the case of reprographic reproduction in accordance with
the terms of licences issued by the Copyright Licensing Agency. Enquiries
concerning reproduction outside those terms should be sent to the publishers.

•

Matador
9 Priory Business Park
Kibworth Beauchamp
Leicestershire LE8 0RX, UK
Tel: (+44) 116 279 2299
Fax: (+44) 116 279 2277
Email: books@troubador.co.uk
Web: www.troubador.co.uk/matador

ISBN 978 1780884 899

British Library Cataloguing in Publication Data.
A catalogue record for this book is available from the British Library.

**Matador** is an imprint of Troubador Publishing Ltd

# R.A.I.D
# RAPID ACTION INITIATED DEFENCE

## MODERN SELF DEFENCE &
## CONFLICT MANAGEMENT

### TREMAINE KENT

H2H Defence.co.uk
Modern Self Defence & Conflict Management

IMPORTANT NOTE: The author and publishers cannot accept any responsibility for and prosecutions or proceedings brought or instituted against any person or body as a result of the use or misuse of any concept described in this book or any loss, injury or damage caused thereby.

All H2H training programs and methodologies such as R.A.I.D. Rapid Action Initiated Defence, S.A.F.E.R. personal security model, S.T.O.P. conflict management model, H.E.L.P. threat assessment and C.O.P.E options model are protected intellectual property. All texts, artwork and trademarks are copyright © H2H Defence Limited 2008/9. No unauthorised reproduction.

# CONTENTS

# R.A.I.D.

# R.A.I.D Defence Cycle / Rapid Action Initiated Defence

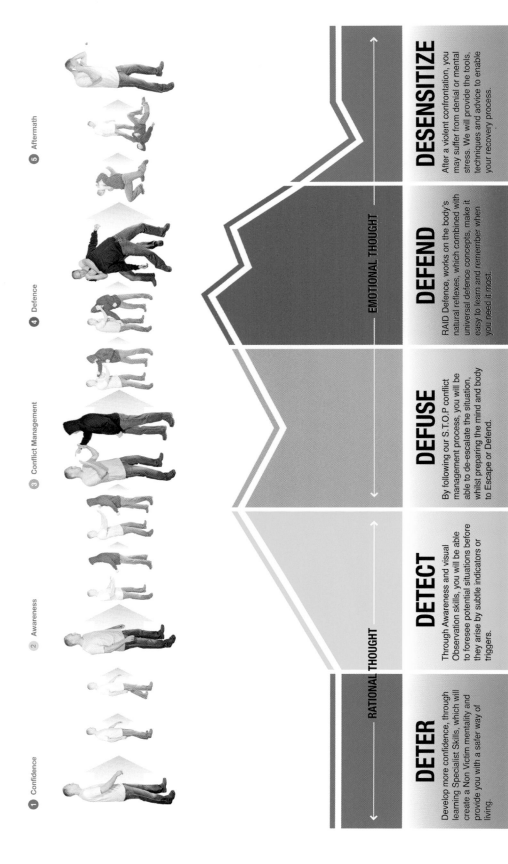

① Confidence  ② Awareness  ③ Conflict Management  ④ Defence  ⑤ Aftermath

## DETER

Develop more confidence, through learning Specialist Skills, which will create a Non Victim mentality and provide you with a safer way of living.

## DETECT

Through Awareness and visual Observation skills, you will be able to foresee potential situations before they arise by subtle indicators or triggers.

## DEFUSE

By following our S.T.O.P conflict management process, you will be able to de-escalate the situation, whilst preparing the mind and body to Escape or Defend.

## DEFEND

RAID Defence, works on the body's natural reflexes, which combined with universal defence concepts, make it easy to learn and remember when you need it most.

## DESENSITIZE

After a violent confrontation, you may suffer from denial or mental stress. We will provide the tools, techniques and advice to enable your recovery process.

← RATIONAL THOUGHT →        ← EMOTIONAL THOUGHT →

← PRE-ASSAULT (PRO-ACTIVE) →        ← ASSAULT (RE-ACTIVE) →        ← POST-ASSAULT (ACTIVE) →

© 2008 to H2H Defence & CTR Services Ltd

** This picture represents the processes of escalation from 1 to 5 of a physical confrontation unfolding

# R.A.I.D RAPID ACTION INITIATED DEFENCE

## ACKNOWLEDGEMENTS

**Richard Dimitri**
Senshido, a true inspiration and personal friend, contributed to the development of this book.

**Steve Webster**
East Coast Karate, working to make a better future for all.

**Adrian Kent & Carla Saunders**
To my brother for helping build a dream and my beloved Carla for helping me grow.

**My Special Forces Unit In Iraq**
The team that pressure tested the system from a hostile environment.

**Steve Collins**
PS5 & REACT Tactical Solutions for his weapons awareness program.

**Jim Wagner**
Reality-Based Personal Protection that enabled me to discover pre and post conflict.

**Geoff Thompson & Peter Consterdine**.
For my personal development

## CERTIFICATION & ASSOCIATION

The R.A.I.D system has been approved by an awarding body and delivered through CTR High Risk Security & Investigations Services Limited which is the sponsor company to H2H Defence Limited. This sponsorship and association creates the perfect learning and qualification environment.

CTR Services...
The Intelligent Approach to Security

We all know that violence is on the increase! You only have to watch television and read the newspapers, with gang cultures, rapes, murders and armed assaults being pushed to the front of the news. Society is becoming vicious and hard. Who is to blame for this increase? Well, we can all point the finger at someone else, but the truth of the matter is that we are all responsible in our own way and even though the national statistics say otherwise it is not getting any better.

## "R.A.I.D. IS NOT GENDER, PHYSICAL PROWESS, AGE OR SIZE DEPENDANT"

Most people are terrified of becoming a victim and apathy seems to be the only defence which dominates people's thoughts. Some individuals take up traditional martial arts to fill the void of knowledge. However, for those of you who have traditional martial arts experience, think about the last self-defence technique you did in class, do you honestly think you could perform that at 4am when you are tired? Or will the technique taught be adaptable to a street, alleyway, car, underground car park or elevator etc? Or will the technique work against a knife attack when it is being thrust at you repeatedly from all angles fast? Or will you be able to stand up in a court of law and defend yourself to prove your innocence without court room survival training?

If the answers are negative you need to have a rethink of your goals of training.

You don't have to have years of experience to be able to defend yourself against today's violent society. R.A.I.D. is not gender, physical prowess, age or size dependant. The answer is simple, if you want to increase your survivability and become safer within a violent confrontation, the self-defence and personal protection training you choose needs to include personal security and protection, conflict management, fear management, pre and post assault training as well as the physical assault elements of defence. Unfortunately, traditional arts severely undermine pre and post assault training and focus on technical applications. These are in direct conflict with our reactive response parts of the brain (startle to flinch) not to mention the lack of conceptual approaches to tactical and strategic defence methodologies.

**So welcome to R.A.I.D.**

# R.A.I.D DEFENCE CYCLE
## RAPID ACTION INITIATED DEFENCE

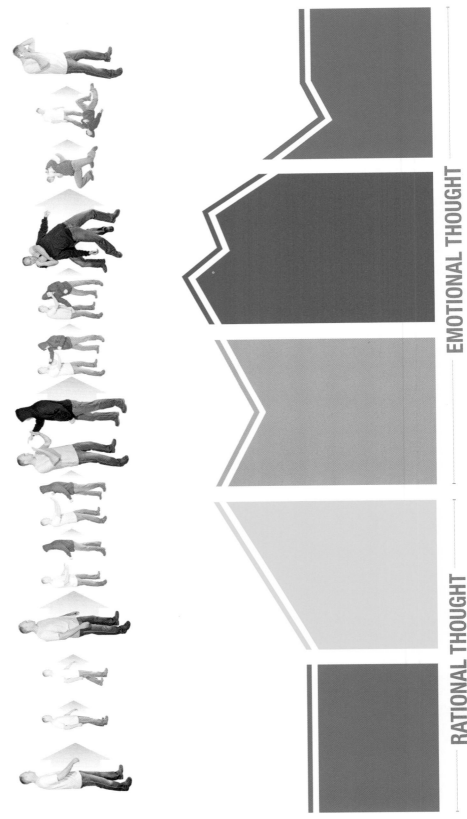

RATIONAL THOUGHT

EMOTIONAL THOUGHT

| 1. CONFIDENCE | 2. AWARENESS | 3. CONFLICT MANAGEMENT | 4. DEFENCE | 5. AFTERMATH |
|---|---|---|---|---|
| **DETER** | **DETECT** | **DEFUSE** | **DEFEND** | **DESENSITIZE** |
| DEVELOP MORE CONFIDENCE THROUGH LEARNING SPECIALIST SKILLS, WHICH WILL CREATE A NON VICTIM MENTALITY AND PROVIDE YOU WITH A SAFER WAY OF LIVING | THROUGH AWARENESS AND VISUAL OBSERVATION SKILLS, YOU WILL BE ABLE TO FORESEE POTENTIAL SITUATIONS BEFORE THEY ARISE BY SUBTLE INDICATORS OR TRIGGERS | BY FOLLOWING OUR S.T.O.P CONFLICT MANAGEMENT PROCESS, YOU WILL BE ABLE TO DE-ESCALATE THE SITUATION, WHILST PREPARING THE MIND AND BODY TO ESCAPE OR DEFEND | R.A.I.D. DEFENCE, WORKS ON THE BODY'S NATURAL REFLEXES WHICH, COMBINED WITH UNIVERSAL DEFENCE CONCEPTS, MAKE IT EASY TO LEARN AND REMEMBER WHEN YOU NEED IT MOST | AFTER A VIOLENT CONFRONTATION, YOU MAY SUFFER FROM DENIAL OR MENTAL STRESS. WE WILL PROVIDE THE TOOLS, TECHNIQUES AND ADVICE TO ENABLE YOUR RECOVERY PROCESS |

PRE-ASSAULT (PRO-ACTIVE) ——— ASSAULT (RE-ACTIVE) ——— POST-ASSAULT (ACTIVE)

The R.A.I.D. chart has taken over three years to design and is the only complete self-defence process from normal everyday life, through a potential confrontation to the aftermath and back to everyday life. This unique system highlights the five D's of defence, which have been designed to provide you with a 100% defence program and not the 15% of physical defence associated with many other systems or arts.

# DETERRENCE CONFIDENCE

 **RATIONAL THOUGHT PROCESS, SLOW RELEASE OF ADRENALINE**

 **60 – 80 BPM NORMAL HEARTRATE**

## KNOWLEDGE DISPELS FEAR – AND PROVIDES CONFIDENCE TO EMPOWER YOU

Have you wondered why people are victims and others are not? Well the way you present yourself to the world and whether you are security conscious or not has a lot to do with it.

Deterrence is the key to the R.A.I.D. system and you have heard the saying "prevention is better than the cure". This is the time to be proactive and strategic in your pre-assault training. With the correct specialized training you will gain the correct specialist knowledge to give you confidence, which in turn will show in your physical behaviour.

This whole module is about personal protection, how to implement security parameters and procedures, whilst at home, work, in the car and out on the street by following a colour coding awareness process. You will learn about your belief systems and how they affect your defensive thinking and views towards life. You will also discover the psychological and physiological effects of fear and how your mind and body reacts to external violent stimulus. Like all foundations this module provides the building blocks for further discovery of personal protection defence.

# DETECTION AWARENESS

 **RATIONAL & EMOTIONAL PROCESSES SEARCH FOR IDEAS. FIRST ADRENALINE DUMP**

 **80 - 115 BPM FINE MOTOR SKILLS FADE**

## IF YOU HAVE KNOWLEDGE OF VIOLENCE AND YOU CAN IDENTIFY A POTENTIAL SITUATION BY OBSERVATION AND AWARENESS – YOU STAND A BETTER CHANCE IN PREVENTING IT

This is the first module of reactive assault training and one that seems to be over looked or not emphasized enough in training. Many individuals that have been in a violent situation seem to forget how it started or what led to their unfortunate attack.

In this module you will discover how to detect potential situations, before they take form. You will learn about the types of attacks and

attackers so that you know how to recognize them when presented to you.

The best way for you to learn this, is to place you in the attackers shoes and get you to study how they choose their victims. You will learn observation and awareness skills which allow you to detect subtle indicators and triggers people show when acting in a certain manner.

# DEFUSE CONFLICT MANAGEMENT

 **EMOTIONAL PROCESSES AFFECTS SYMPATHETIC NERVOUS SYSTEM. SECOND ADRENALIN DUMP**

 **115 – 145 BPM COMPLEX MOTOR SKILLS FADE**

## IF THE ATTACKER WILL TALK - HE MAY PRESENT THE ABILITY FOR YOU TO WALK

The second module within reactive assault is defusing or what is known as conflict management. When the situation has escalated and you have not been able to avoid it, a lot of people seem to find it difficult to communicate in a stressful situation and end up making it worse. If you find yourself in this position you will be feeling the effects of emotional adrenalin and physiological change, like accelerated heart and respiration rate, dry mouth, etc.

This module is very important and is the choices part of your defence strategy through understanding the law and Means Opportunity and Intent (MOI) use of force ladder, because we provide you with a tactical conflict management process called "STOP" which guides you through a situation step by step. You will learn active listening and de-escalation skills to enable the reintroduction of rational thought processing so that you can make rational decisions or choices.

# DEFEND DEFENCE

 **EMOTIONAL PROCESSES TRANSFERS SIGNALS TO EXCRETE THIRD ADRENALINE DUMP**

 **145 – 175+ BPM GROSS MOTOR SKILLS & STARTLE TO FLINCH STARTS**

## MAKE YOUR NATURAL DEFENCE SUIT YOU – AND NOT SUIT YOUR ATTACKER

Defence is the last resort and last module within reactive assault, as all attempts to get away have been negated and de-escalation and conflict management skills have failed. In this module you will learn the physical elements of the tactical "COPE" process which allows you to reflexively cope with any physical assault you may encounter. The module is split into understandable segments starting with:

### Knowledge Based
The knowledge based elements help establish an understanding about the body and what it can and can't do and what happens to you when it is attacked. You will also learn anatomy of defence, target areas of the anatomy and tools of defence, so that you can protect yourself scientifically and economically through personal experience and self understanding of the anatomy.

### Physical Based
The physical based element is split into four:

1. Basic Combat Arts: The first part is to understand what and how your body can protect yourself. Basic Combat Arts (BCA) will enable you to learn not only different defences but also the pros and cons for each. This also provides body conditioning, fight fitness and assertiveness development.

2. Minimum Force: Which follows the next level from conflict management and includes attitude adjustment, breakaways and many more defence methodologies for use in the eyes of the law.

3. Reasonable Force: The next physical base element is reasonable force, where you will learn different ranges of defence and most common attack concepts such as ABC of chokes, sucker punch mentality and many more defence tactics.

4. Force Continuum: The final physical base element will teach you how to defend yourself against improvised weapons defence, edged weapons or knife threat and attack defence, long weapon defence and firearms threat defence tactics.

# DESENSITIZE AFTERMATH

 EMOTIONAL BECOMES RATIONAL
AND MIND COMES BACK TO NORMAL

 145 – 80 BPM BODY AND HEARTRATE
RETURNS TO NORMAL

## ONLY THROUGH ACCEPTANCE AND UNDERSTANDING WILL YOU LEARN, DEVELOP AND MOVE FORWARD, WITH YOUR LIFE

After a confrontation either mentally or physically, you will always be affected by the post traumatic effects such as denial or even legal or social consequence. This is the last module within the R.A.I.D. Cycle and is the post assault phase. During this module you will learn on the scene first aid, known as self triage, which helps you to get back your rational thought whilst checking your body for serious wounds. You will also learn courtroom survival strategies so that you can defend yourself in court as you did on the street. You will also discover coping strategies for post traumatic stress disorder (PTSD). This module is again overlooked but it is the only true way of learning from experience positively so that you may make a full recovery.

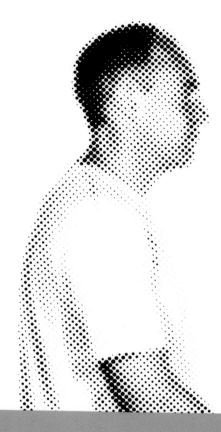

# DETER

# R.A.I.D Defence Cycle / Rapid Action Initiated Defence

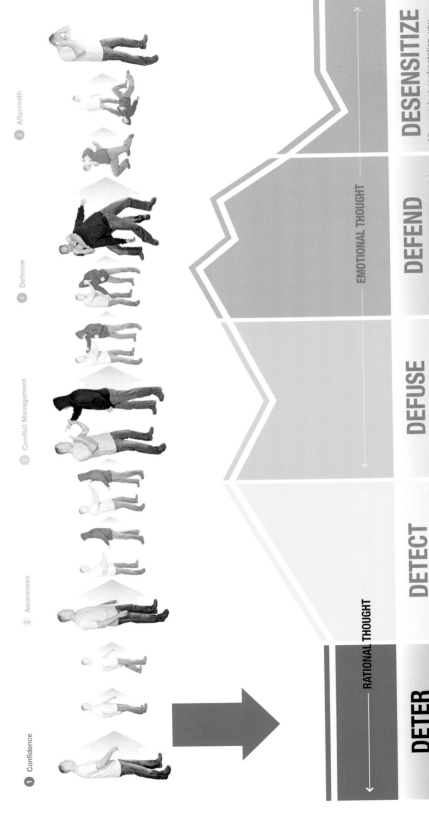

1 Confidence  2 Awareness  3 Conflict Management  4 Defence  5 Aftermath

**RATIONAL THOUGHT**

**EMOTIONAL THOUGHT**

## DETER

Develop more confidence, through learning Specialist Skills, which will create a Non Victim mentality and provide you with a safer way of living.

## DETECT

Through Awareness and visual Observation skills, you will be able to foresee potential situations before they arise by subtle indicators or triggers.

## DEFUSE

By following our S.T.O.P conflict management process, you will be able to de-escalate the situation, whilst preparing the mind and body to Escape or Defend.

## DEFEND

RAID Defence, works on the body's natural reflexes, which combined with universal defence concepts, make it easy to learn and remember when you need it most.

## DESENSITIZE

After a violent confrontation, you may suffer from denial or mental stress. We will provide the tools, techniques and advice to enable your recovery process.

PRE-ASSAULT (PRO-ACTIVE) →

ASSAULT (RE-ACTIVE)

POST-ASSAULT (ACTIVE)

** This picture represents the processes of escalation from 1 to 5 of a physical confrontation unfolding

© 2008 to H2H Defence & CTR Services Ltd

# WELCOME TO DETERRENCE

**Founder/Chief Instructor**
Mr Tremaine Kent

Designed by Tremaine Kent, this module is the key as you have heard the saying "prevention is better than the cure". This is the time to be proactive and strategic in your training. With the correct training you will gain the correct knowledge to give you confidence which in turn will show in your physical behaviour. This whole module is about personal protection, how to implement security parameters and procedures, whilst at home, work, in the car and out on the street by following a colour coding awareness system. You will learn about your belief systems and how they affect your defensive thinking and views. You will also discover the psychological and physiological effects of fear and how your mind and body reacts to external violent stimulus.

Like all foundations this module provides the building blocks for further discovery of personal protective defence.

# BELIEF SYSTEMS

## "BE SURE TO CHOOSE WHAT YOU BELIEVE AND KNOW WHY YOU BELIEVE IT, BECAUSE IF YOU DON'T CHOOSE YOUR BELIEFS, YOU MAY BE CERTAIN THAT SOME BELIEF AND PROBABLY NOT A VERY CREDIBLE ONE WILL CHOOSE YOU."

### What is a belief system?

Belief systems involve all aspects of human existence, from the perspective that the positive and negative vision of all reality is the product of consciousness. A person's beliefs define the limits of their experiences within this realm, which means that if you believe you cannot do something you won't be able to. If you study a traditional art or combat sport for some years and are asked to fight multiple attackers, unless you truly believe you can do it, no amount of technical teachings will allow you to meet the challenge.

What is certain is that if we don't develop consciousness on our own beliefs we may fall into or take on others.

If you take the belief systems of many people before the 15th century, if you believed anything other than the world was flat you were classed as a heretic and executed by the church. Through consciousness, experience and knowledge some of the greatest explorers and exceptional individuals changed our beliefs to what we now acknowledge: "the world being round".

### Creating the winning belief system

When new students are asked can they defend themselves or do they believe they can defend themselves against a violent person, the answer is normally always "I think I can". This belief system cannot be changed by technical instruction alone. The student needs to change their consciousness by prioritizing their survival mindset.

### Survival Mindset

When you use empowerment words and start to create a winning inner coach, you need to put situations into realistic perspective and appreciate all variables. For instance, if you fear something happening to your children and you were asked a hypothetical question such as, you come home from work and you find that a huge 6 foot 6 inch man is attacking your children what would you do? A lot of you

would say "I would kill him" and that you would fight hard. Now if we take the same attacker but the attack doesn't include your children and the attack is against you, could you defend yourself? The answer would be much different and you would get the response of "possibly" or "I don't know". Well this is ridiculous because the attack is the same and the reason being, who will look after your children if you are killed? I often ask

many bodyguards/protection operatives, who is the most important person in the team, the client or protection operative? The responses I get back are mixed but frequently the client is the important one. How can this be, surely the protection operative is the most important person, because if he is not there the client is dead anyway. The method for training the survival mindset is through our GLF training sessions which takes you beyond the normal parameters of a fight scenario to build up your mental blueprinting, stamina, emotional interrupt, endurance and are covered later in the course.

## Why are belief systems important in self defence?

The reason is that the mind navigates the body and unless you truly believe you can defend yourself the body will not be navigated to perform to the best of its capabilities. To give you an example that you can try yourself, close your eyes and close your mouth, suck all the saliva in and swallow so your mouth is considerably dry. Now imagine picking up a chopped lemon and bite into it with your teeth and imagine the feel and taste of the sharp citrus lemon flavour; by now your mouth is full of saliva and very watery, this is because the mind is using your senses and navigating the physiological effects and excreting saliva from your imagination, which shows that if your mind believes something to be true, then the body will follow.

## THINK POINT DETERRENCE 1

**1.1 CLARIFY WHAT A BELIEF SYSTEM IS AND HOW IMPORTANT IT IS IN SELF DEFENCE**
**1.2 EXPLAIN YOUR BELIEF SYSTEM IN RELATION TO YOUR OWN SELF DEFENCE**

SEE YOUR INSTRUCTOR FOR WORKSHEET (IF YOU ARE TAKING EXAM)

# FEAR MANAGEMENT

## "FEAR IS A NEGATIVE THOUGHT THAT IS LEAD BY EMOTION WHICH TRIGGERS BIOLOGICAL CHANGES IN OUR BODY."

### What is Fear?

Fear exists in every day life and you have to deal with your own internal and external fears regularly. Fear can be described by an acronym of itself:

### FALSE EVIDENCE APPEARING REAL

which is the way your consciousness plays out the outcome of a situation in a negative way. If you take a driving exam for instance, prior to the exam you worry, because you fear the fact that you may potentially fail. The way you eventually overcome this fear is by knowledge through study and the more study you do the better prepared and confident you feel, which in turn reduces the fear of the exam. To equate fear to defence, the more you understand defence strategies the more confident you become when dealing with situations and the better your ability to reduce and minimise fear.

Fear itself is an emotion which has three elements, emotional, psychological and biological each of which are directly linked to the other through human response to stimulus.

To better understand the three elements in a heightened stressful situation, the emotion (feeling) cannot cope with the stress and creates psychological (thinking) fear in which you will think negatively about the outcome or consequence of the situation. Your biological response to this stimulus is an elevated heart and breath rate, vasoconstriction of the blood vessels to extremities and the stimulation of the sympathetic nervous system that releases adrenaline into the blood stream to cope with the stimulus. This release of adrenaline is the physical symptom which at times can be mistaken for fear and creates panic.

### How does the mind navigate the body?

As the mind navigates the body and every mental and physical action or process you do stems from the mind, if you cannot control your fears you will be disadvantaged in the physical defence we use. This is why fear management training is essential in your defence training. An example of this would be if you are a runner and you wake up in the morning it's not your legs that decide to take you for a training run, it's your mind that decides you should run. The connection between the emotional brain and biological action stems from the central nervous system, which is made up of two elements: the brain which is the thought process and the spinal cord which sends the messages to the relevant parts of the body to take action.

### Types of Fear

There have been many types of fear documented for self defence but we will consider five main fear processes. Each one will provide an introduction, explanation and a management process so that you can clearly understand the emotional, psychological and biological effects of each. A note to point out is that any of these processes can happen at any time and they don't all necessarily follow suit. The R.A.I.D. system, as previously mentioned, is broken down into the five D's of defence, which allows you to clearly see how the emotional and biological fear processes work in parallel with the situational stimulus.

# PRE-ASSAULT FEAR

## Introduction

Pre-assault fear or everyday fear are the fears you face on a daily basis. It may be an exam, interview or social acceptance within a group or work environment. It is the worries you have daily which you generally are able to deal with quickly and without consequence.

## What is Pre-Assault Fear?

We have established that fear is emotionally driven which affects us biologically and when we think of all the information we hold for dealing with violence we have the external fears of consequence and anticipation of the outcome. Whether it is being afraid of pain, death, rape, law, the police etc. This fear over a certain period of time affects us biologically and we produce a slow release of adrenaline through the autonomic sympathetic nervous system. The emotional inertia caused by anticipation or consequence can lead to stress which may effect our sleep and eating patterns.

## Pre-Assault Fear Management

The best management of pre-assault fear is knowledge and understanding. If you negate apathy and your attitude towards potential violence is acceptance, and you gain experience and knowledge of the consequence from a legal standpoint of reasonable and justifiable force, you will understand how to prevent, defuse and defend a violent attack. Therefore for the emotional psychological effects will not stimulate the biological effects, which in turn will not stimulate the sympathetic nervous system and adrenaline release.

---

**1. Emotional**
The fear of consequence and anticipation creates stress.

**2. Biological**
Sympathetic Nervous System that excretes a slow amount of adrenaline.

1. _____

2. _____

 **60 - 80 BPM**

# PRIMARY ASSAULT FEAR

## Introduction

This is the situation you find yourself in when your awareness is not present and you fail to identify a violent situation, or that you have judged a situation wrong and the speed of escalation is so fast that the biological system goes into over drive, and you panic and freeze up. You may also go into this fear if pre-assault fear wasn't present and there was no lead to the attack. This is also known as:

FIGHT OR FLIGHT SYNDROME
WOW FACTOR
ADRENALINE DUMP

### What is Primary Assault Fear?

Due to the speed of escalation the heart and respiration rate accelerates and biologically stimulates the sympathetic nervous system which dumps adrenaline into the system. The mind then confuses and mistakes this biological change for fear and causes the body to freeze up. The physical symptoms of this biological change range from a pounding heart rate, dry mouth, shaking of the extremities, tunnelled vision, a heavy feeling in the stomach etc.

### Primary Assault Fear Management

Obviously the main point here is to not only develop the necessary Awareness and Assumption rule skills which are covered later, but also consciously tell yourself "this is a normal response to a situation" and try to interrupt your thought process of fear by using the COPE options module covered later.

### 1. Attacker
Due to lack of awareness or reading the situation wrong the attacker initiates their attack without you being prepared.

### 2. Biological
Heart & Respiration rate initiates the sympathetic nervous system and overloads the body with adrenaline.

### 3. Emotional
The adrenaline is mistaken for fear and the body freezes.

1. ————————
2. ————————
3. ————————

 **80 – 145 BPM**

# SECONDARY ASSAULT FEAR

### Introduction
This may occur when you are trying to de-escalate or defend against a situation and you find that you are engulfed in your actions. Then unexpectedly the situation changes and the attacker draws an edged weapon, which you don't see until it cuts you or they do something completely random but dangerous to you.

### What is Secondary Assault Fear?
Like the primary assault fear, this secondary assault fear is biological first in that your body initiates another adrenaline dump through the autonomic sympathetic nervous system to protect the areas of the body that have possibly become injured. The psychological brain tries to interpret what has happened and analyses the situation. Sometimes you may not realise you have been cut until the very end as the biological adrenaline is masking pain and sensation.

### Secondary Assault Fear Management
Initially it is imperative to stop the defence and analyse what has happened as this will surely seal your doom. During training it is good practice to conduct the one to five training drills within scenario replications. Again you should always defend reflexively so that your awareness is not focused allowing you to see changes in the attack.

### 1. Attacker
During the assault and due to lack of awareness or reading the situation wrong, the attacker draws an edged weapon and cuts you.

### 2. Biological
The sympathetic nervous system boosts the body with adrenaline.

### 3. Emotional
The brain tries to analyse what has happened, and you freeze.

1.
2.
3.

 115 - 175 BPM

# TERTIARY ASSAULT FEAR

### Introduction
This is when you have a strategic or tactical plan formulated by following our COPE options module and your body has prepared biologically for action. Then you are taken by surprise and something different happens instead, which negates your plan and destroys your emotional and biological systems.

### What is Tertiary Assault Fear?
Your parasympathetic nervous system is dampening the sympathetic nervous system and slowing the release of adrenaline as you mentally and psychologically reduce the fear. Then when the situation goes in a different direction you suffer a sudden emotional fear which causes hesitation and another adrenaline dump and increased heart and respiration rate.

### Tertiary Fear Management
Even though you feel confident in the outcome, never stop assuming (covered later) and following the S.T.O.P. conflict management module and COPE options module (covered later), this will keep you reflexively adapting to the environment and situation
as it changes.

**1. Emotional & Biological**
You have prepared your strategic and tactical plan and your biological system is prepared thus reducing fear.

**2. Attacker**
Then out of the blue you are attacked from behind.

**3. Biological**
The biological system crashes and the body dumps adrenaline again.

1. _____

2. _____

3. _____

 115 – 175 BPM

# POST-ASSAULT FEAR

## Introduction
This is when the confrontation is over and your mind and body have started to calm down.
You are able to reflect on what happened, how it happened and all the other considerations you will have internally and externally.

## What is Post-Assault Fear?
Internal: once you have survived the attack your emotional thinking starts to come back to rational thinking and your parasympathetic nervous system calms the sympathetic nervous system and slows your heart and respiration rate down. You will most certainly experience post traumatic effects as seen many times from soldiers in high risk conflict zones and you will still produce a steady flow of adrenaline.

Denial, which we cover later

Depression, sorrow, sadness, withdrawal from friends, social gatherings, work etc

Anger, rage, frustration aimed at everyone, religion and even themselves.

Negotiation with their morals *"please if only. I will never steal, drink too much etc."*

Acceptance: the final stage where they will be able to free themselves from the feelings of the event.

External: you will always also consider the legal aspect of your actions and worry or fear that you will be in trouble with the law and police, again through questions such as: "What if I...?", "Could I have...?" etc.

## Post-Assault Fear Management
Internal As soon as the event has happened you should conduct self triage (covered later), which should also be practiced in training in scenario replications. Once you have time to regain some peace of mind you should be prepared for the physical and mental effects and as difficult as it may seem, try to be optimistic. You may need to seek professional counselling and advice, also to surround yourself with family and friends that provide comfort and security.

External: by training in post conflict scenarios and gaining an understanding of the laws relating to self defence, the consequence from the law will give you confidence and in some cases aid with the internal effects suffered.

---

### 1. Emotional & Rational
Your emotional thought starts to come back to rational thought.

### 2. Biological
The parasympathetic nervous system starts to slow things down, but allowing a small slow adrenaline stream into the body.

1._____

2._____

 **145 - 80 BPM**

# CONCLUSION

To sum it all up the equation to remember
is the following:

**PSYCHOLOGICAL FEAR = EMOTIONAL FEAR = WHICH STIMULATES THE SYMPATHETIC NERVOUS SYSTEM = WHICH EXCRETES ADRENALIN = BIOLOGICAL FEAR.**

Always remember that Fear can also be a good thing if it is active fear, however the fear we talk about can destroy you that's why we need to understand it.

"Knowledge dispels fear"

# NOTES (PLEASE USE THIS AREA FOR NOTES)

# APATHY & DENIAL

### Apathy

Apathy creates victim mentality and those apathetic people usually end up as a national statistic once in their lives. The common sentences used by apathetic people are:

**"THIS WILL NEVER HAPPEN TO ME"**

**"I LIVE IN A SAFE AREA"**

**"PEOPLE, WHO LOOK FOR IT, FIND IT, NOT ME"**

These are but a few sentences used and through our understanding of belief systems these views replicate in our attitudes. The reason we address apathy is to change the direction of thinking and create awareness that there is the potential that we may face a violent confrontation in our lives, so that when faced with a situation, the shock is manageable due to the acceptance of the possibility.

### Denial

Denial is in two forms: the first is denial in conflict, which normally follows apathetic individuals and whilst being attacked their body's freeze whilst their thoughts tell them:

**"I CAN'T BELIEVE THIS IS HAPPENING TO ME"**

**"IF I PRETEND IT ISN'T THERE, IT WILL GO AWAY"**

Then there is denial after the event which also has the same process of thoughts:

**"WHY ME"**

**"I SHOULD HAVE… COULD HAVE…? ETC"**

This form of denial has many associations with it as it goes hand in hand with post traumatic stress disorder, PTSD. Even after an attack when you have extracted, defended or merely survived, your body will start to slow down and try and make sense of the situation, as well as remaining alert for another potential attack.

---

## THINK POINT DETERRENCE 2

**2.1 EXPLAIN THE FIVE TYPES OF FEAR**
**2.2 EVALUATE APATHY AND DENIAL**

SEE YOUR INSTRUCTOR FOR WORKSHEET (IF YOU ARE TAKING EXAM)

# S.A.F.E.R GUIDE TO PERSONAL SECURITY

### What is S.A.F.E.R.

This personal security system has been designed for the close protection (bodyguard) security sector and is taught as part of the new Security Industry Authority (SIA) licensed program. The S.A.F.E.R. acronym originates from the Royal Military Police close protection instruction and now is used by many commercial protection operatives, in the UK and overseas. The S.A.F.E.R. guide is merely a tool of principles which are aimed at changing your frame of mind. They will not present you with the ultimate solution, but if you apply them as guidelines you will greatly improve your level of security, they are as follows:

## SAFER

**S**ITUATIONAL AWARENESS
**A**VOID ROUTINE
**F**OLLOW SECURITY
**E**XERCISE COMMON SENSE
**R**EMAIN ANONYMOUS

### S – Situational awareness

Accept a threat exists, remember apathy is no excuse. Be vigilant at work and leisure; be suspicious, cautious/paranoid in your approach, even when you are not working. As you go about your normal lives you must be constantly aware of your surroundings and environment, you should be looking for the abnormal, the new face in the neighbourhood, the car parked in the same place with different drivers. All these signs should heighten your alertness and you should be questioning why? Looking for other possible indicators and thinking of your plan of action to either confirm your suspicions or discount the matter. Many of these areas will be covered in more detail in later modules.

### A – Avoid routine

Change your routes and timings. Routines kill as the expression goes, however to change your natural daily routine will provide some degree of unpredictability. The threat will usually go for the easy target with guaranteed success. They will first of all look for and identify their victim's habits and lifestyle. If you present them with a predictable routine you have done the majority of their work for them. You must be careful in the following areas:

**Timings and locations:** some of these you have no influence over, such as going to work in the morning, you can only vary timings so much before they become impractical and tedious.

Others you can vary, especially socially such as bars, restaurants, etc; which highlights another important point and that is the routine set by others which you may fall into.

**Routes:** if you travel to work every day you must try to use as many different routes as possible. This is very difficult to do in some areas especially at the beginning and end of the journey where you normally converge onto a known destination. As well as varying your routes you can vary your mode of transport, i.e. running, cycling or vehicle, this will probably give you more choice of routes as well as varying timings.

## F – Follow security procedures

Establish procedures for home, office, family etc. Make sure they are not ridiculously strict and then follow them. We will cover this later.

## E – Exercise common sense and initiative

Do not panic, use any means at your disposal to counter a threat (this will be covered later in Defuse & Defend modules). All of these principles and the procedures that follow must be applied with common sense otherwise they will interfere with your every day life and the more they interfere, the more you will be tempted to take short-cuts or even drop them altogether. You must also use our initiative to overcome any shortcomings in security or lack of equipment. You do not want to become paranoid or turn into "Walter Mitties" but you must go about your daily life in a state of "relaxed awareness" carrying out simple drills and ready to take the necessary action to deal with any incidents.

## R – Remain anonymous or show strength

Low profile with ex-directory phone numbers, dress conservatively, not provocatively and do not display jewellery or cash when you go out. If you look at wealthy individuals, the ones that are exceptionally wealthy always seem to stay under the radar of the media. This is because they keep themselves to themselves and remain anonymous. All of these principles are normal common sense stuff. You should also remain confident but blend into the crowd. If anonymity is impossible, make the attacker believe an attack would not succeed. Show alertness, confidence and your awareness to them.

## THINK POINT DETERRENCE 3

**3.1 SUMMARISE THE KEY AREAS OF THE SAFER GUIDE TO PERSONAL SAFETY.**

SEE YOUR INSTRUCTOR FOR WORKSHEET (IF YOU ARE TAKING EXAM)

# PERSONAL PROTECTION SECURITY

### What is Personal Protection & Security

Personal protection is the ability to implement security procedures in your daily life and more importantly to be able to follow them. We have discovered the S.A.F.E.R. guide of personal security and we refer to the importance of following security procedures. This session will give you a conceptual awareness for implementing your own personal security procedures. This is by no means an exhaustive list and you can find more information or advice from your local services or implement some of the tips we provide. The protective advice on the following subjects will be introduced then followed by a pictorial representation of the environment:

### Home Security

Even though you can lower your alertness and vigilance because you are in a place of sanctuary, unless you follow good security you are as vulnerable as being outside. This element is designed to give you ideas for securing your home or residence.

### Street Security

Being aware whilst on the street is very important and you should consider personal security at all times. Dependant on certain factors such as time of day, environment and situation etc, you may have to step up or lower your security awareness. This element will focus on personal security on the street and how to implement basic security.

### Vehicle Security

With the benefit of security whilst travelling in a vehicle, it is not without its own security issues. The crimes involving vehicles such as road rage, theft and car jacking should not overwhelm the areas of breakdown and road traffic collisions as these can induce potential incidents. This element provides security advice for drivers of motor cars and riders of motor bikes.

### Public Transport Security

Whether you are on a train, bus or use taxis, some of the main security issues overlap. This element will cover many of the main transport methods and will provide simple proactive security advice for each of them.

### Work Security

When you are at work and in an office, storeroom, warehouse or outside, the security procedures you adopt should be in acceptance with your employer's security policy. The duty of care policy which has been introduced due to the corporate manslaughter bill has seen a dramatic change within businesses, from health and safety for lone workers to security policy and procedures. This element will provide some extra ideas which may aid in better personal security at work.

### Personal Protection Equipment

With today's technological advances, the personal alarms, SOS and tracking systems can aid personal safety without financial ruin. The systems that we will cover have been tried and tested and used by many clients and personnel we have trained and supplied.

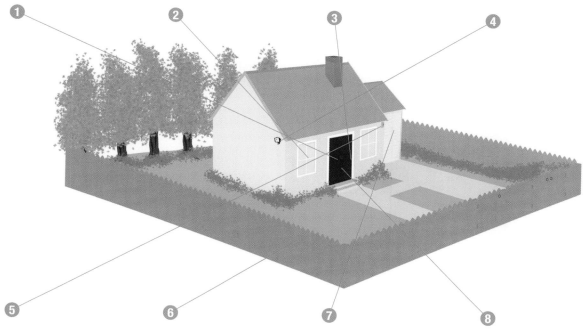

## HOME SECURITY

### 1. Doors
- Make sure all doors are secure at all times, even when you are in the home.
- Try to have doors which are certified by British standards.
- Use special film on glass or laminate door panels to make them secure.
- Door frames should be secured and the doors no less than 44mm in thickness.
- Try to have five lever mortis deadlocks to British standards fitted.

### 2. Windows
- Use windows that are British standards.
- Keep windows locked when not in use and ensure when locked that the key is fitted in case of an emergency.
- If you are going to make security alterations to windows, check with the manufacturers first.

### 3. Keys
- Never leave spare keys in convenient places such as under the door mat or flower pot as these places will be checked.

- If you move into a new home ensure that you replace all the locks on the doors and assign new keys.
- Keep a spare set of keys with relatives but don't place any label on them pertaining to the name or address you live at.

### 4. Lights
- Outside lights should be low energy dusk till dawn lights that come on when it's dark. This acts as a deterrent and allows ease of movement outside for you.
- Lights should be fitted above 2.5 meters off the ground below them so that they cannot be tampered with.
- PIR or passive infrared activated lights work on movement and will come on when someone walks in their beam.

### 5. Alarms
- Decide whether you require an audible alarm or a monitored alarm which goes to a control centre. Be aware that police will only respond to audible alarms if it has been verified, so unless you are on a neighbourhood watch scheme

and a neighbour phones the police they may not respond. Where as a central control centre will respond first, verify and call police whilst they are dealing with the situation.
- Any system you buy needs to be certified to British standards (wire free) or the new European standard.

### 6. Fences
- Install strong fencing and gates as this is your first line of defence.
- Bushes and thorny hedges on your side of the fence create an excellent deterrent.
- Use gravel as it is noisy under foot.

### 7. Garages
- Garages and sheds are often full of expensive goods so don't ignore them and give them the same security.
- If you have electric roller shutter doors and the garage is connected to the side of the house, have an isolator switch fitted inside the house so that you may turn off the electrics to the doors when you are in the home.

### 8. Mail, Telephone and Internet

- Try to have the mail box fitted to a secure container on the side of the house wall next to the door with no letter box.
- For tighter security you can purchase a PO Box number and have letters redirected to your house so that they remain secure.
- If you have a home phone number make it ex-directory so that it is not listed under your name.
- Never give out information that someone will be able to find you offline.
- Use virus software and if you are banking online then we suggest some sort of robo form which allows you to store encrypted passwords that fill online bank details at the click of a button securely.
- If you use a wireless network make sure it is secure and if you have data on the computer then secure it into a secure locker on the hard drive which is password protected.

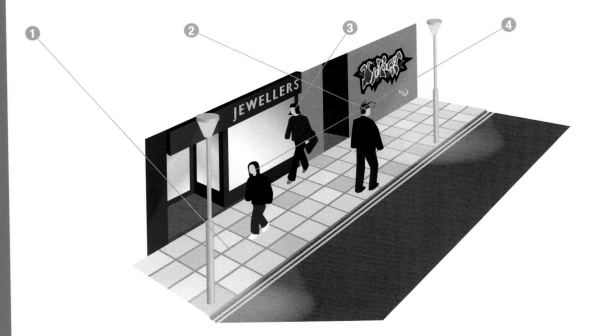

## STREET SECURITY

### 1. The Street

- If you are walking home at night then use a personal attack alarm or spray.

- Make sure someone is always aware of your whereabouts and routes at night.

- If you are carrying something make sure it doesn't get in your way and is not attached to you so it can be discarded.

- Keep all valuables on the inside pockets close to the body and zipped or fastened closed. Don't take shortcuts down alleys at night to get home quicker.

- Don't hitch hike or take lifts from people you don't know.

### 2. Men

- Avoid groups of guys and cross over the road if possible to gain an early indication of a potential situation.

- Try to stay in well lit areas.

- Carry a false wallet with a few pounds or notes in so that if you are mugged you can let them have it.

- If you are drinking alcohol then ensure someone is with you who you trust, so designate a driver for the night and pay for their drinks (orange juice).

### 3. Women

- When out try to remain aware of your environment.

- Crowded areas of men may provoke sexual assault so try to keep in areas of other females.

- Try not to wear clothes that may interest attackers, so try to dress conservatively.

- Try to conceal expensive jewellery when on the street.

- Don't leave your drinks unattended as date rape is on the increase.

- Avoid isolated areas, especially ones you don't know.

- Don't wear scarves and items of clothing or bags round the neck that can be pulled.

- Carry an SOS alarm on your mobile phone and keep it in your hand or in your pocket for easy access.

### 4. Children & Teenagers

- Children should not be allowed to wander off when out. Use a child line or a child finder.

- Don't leave children with people you don't know.

- Use tracking systems that are placed in the clothing.

- Ensure teenagers know they have a support structure at home that is open to listening.

- When teenagers go out ensure you fix rules on times and places they can and cannot go.

- Lead by example and try to include them in your lives so they can see how to behave and so that a unified bonding is still in place.

- Offer to pick them up if going out at night.

- Ensure they have communications and that they know how to use the SOS facility.

- If they are sexually active make sure they have condoms and make them aware of STD's.

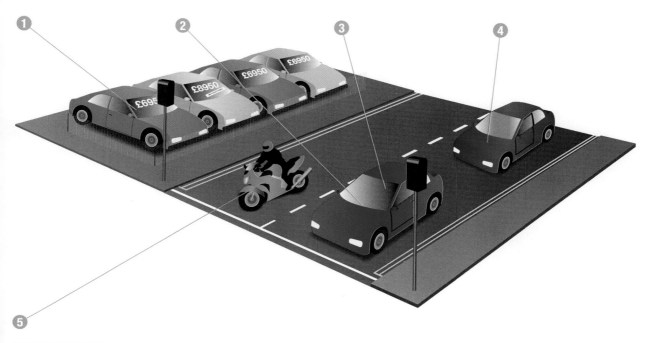

# VEHICLE SECURITY

## 1. Buying and Selling a Vehicle

- Check to make sure the vehicle is not stolen.

- Always arrange to meet the person at their house and not yours.

- Check security etchings for VIM numbers and that they exist in three places on the vehicle.

- Check the documents of ownership and service history and even call the previous owner to confirm its authenticity.

## 2. Motor Cars

### General

- Keep doors locked when travelling and remove all valuables from sight.

- Try to camouflage your gender by having magazines etc in view, which send the message whether you are male or female.

- Ensure the vehicle is road worthy.

- Make sure you always have over half a tank of fuel and spare money in the vehicle.

- Ensure you have a mobile phone and car charger in the vehicle in case of emergencies.

### On the move

- Avoid routine and always vary routes.

- Keep windows closed or open no more than one inch as to stop people leaning in.

- If you see a breakdown or crash report it on your mobile from a safe static area.

- Make sure you have the right equipment in the car for emergencies.

## 3 Vehicle equipment

- Spare wheel should always be checked and maintained.

- Make sure you have a good jack and wheel brace and if you have alloy wheels the correct security nut to unfasten them.

- Try to carry "run-flat foam" which you spray into the wheel as this may allow you to drive to a safe location.

- Carry a small tool set for basic minor repairs.

- Carry a first aid kit and know what the contents include and how to use them.

- Carry a travel bag with spare clothes, a blanket and sleeping bag in case you are stuck in the vehicle.

- Carry two litres of water and some kind of food for emergencies.

- A high visibility vest, gloves, torch, basic tools are all necessary items to be carried.

## 4. Anti Road Rage & Car Jacking

- Keep all windows and doors locked and don't get out of the vehicle at all.

- If you can drive then drive to the nearest safe area such as a police station etc.

- If struck activate your four way flashers and call the police on your mobile.

## 5. Motor Cycles

- Make sure you wear the correct clothing and that you are visible.

- Always use a security device which can inform you if the bike is moved and that can be tracked.

- Always lock the bike to something that cannot be moved and secured to the ground.

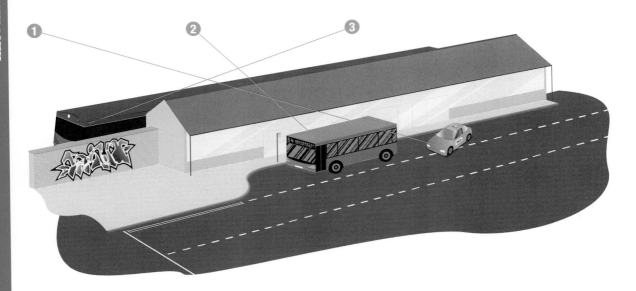

## PUBLIC TRANSPORT SECURITY

### 1. Taxis
Before you travel
- Try to use a reputable taxi firm that you call and comes to pick you up.
- Ensure you know the driver's name.
- If you are out try to use a taxi firm that you know the number of and get them to pick you up from a populated area.

During travel
- Always sit behind the driver.
- Make sure that he knows where you want to be dropped off.
- Ensure the meter is on and that he displays his badge.

Actions to be taken
- Record the driver's information mentally or type into your mobile if you are suspicious.
- If in doubt get out.
- When you get to your destination ask the driver to wait until you have gone inside until he pulls away.

### 2. Bus
General
- Try to stay away from isolated bus stops after dark.
- Try to get to the bus stop with five to ten minuets prior to the bus coming.
- Stay under well lit signs so that people and drivers can see you.
- Use bus stops that are used by other people.

During travel
- If the bus is quiet then sit behind the driver so that he can see you in his mirror.
- Be aware of people listening to your conversations and being overheard.
- Only get off if safe to do so and when the area is well lit.

Actions to be taken
- If you are being harassed on the bus inform the driver who will deal with the situation.
- Don't get into arguments on the bus with other passengers.

### 3. Train
Before you travel
- If travelling late or early morning get someone to see you off.
- Try to stay in areas of groups so that you are not on your own.
- Get all the information you need regarding times and platform before you arrive.
- Try to sort your personal belongings out so you have money and valuables available but secure.

During travel
- Always try to get a carriage that has other people in.
- Be aware of people and luggage and ensure when people get off they take their luggage with them.
- Keep valuables on your person.
- Try not to say too much to people and on the mobile, as people may be listening.

Actions to be taken
- If you are involved in an argument move carriage.
- In the event of an emergency use the emergency stop button and await the conductor.
- Always read the information on emergencies and know where the emergency exits are and how to operate them.

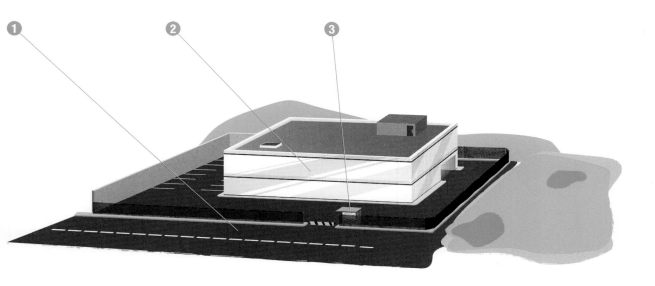

## WORK SECURITY

**1. Going to work**
Travel

- If you drive to work vary your routes and times to avoid routines.

- Make sure your vehicle is road worthy.

- Try to sort out a vehicle permit so that your vehicle can be parked on premises.

- If you bus or train to work, again avoid routine as much as possible, given the travel times of trains and busses.

- Try not to make it obvious what your business is, so keep business material covered up.

- Don't talk about work on public transport as you don't know who is listening.

Arrival

- If you are driving try to park in a secure parking area or on the premises.

- Before you unlock the doors check the area using the mirrors to make sure there is no unfamiliar or individuals that shouldn't be there, waiting for you.

- If you take public transport then ensure you are not being followed.

**2. At work**
During work

- If you work in an office then ensure you have a clean desktop policy which means any sensitive or personal information is locked away if you leave your desk.

- If you have a computer terminal ensure it is password protected and that the monitor doesn't face windows which can be overlooked.

- Any personal information should be kept separate and on person if you share a desk with a co-worker.

**3. Leaving work**
Leaving & Travel

- If you have to lock up and are leaving late make sure you are not being watched and carry your attack alarm on you.

- Check around your vehicle before you enter, to confirm no one is waiting for you.

- If you travel on public transport be aware of your environment.

- Upon returning home check to make sure you weren't followed and lock your vehicle and house door behind you.

# PERSONAL PROTECTION EQUIPMENT (PPE)

## Introduction
Personal protection equipment is only an aid to security and is not intended to be relied on for the first line of defence. The equipment discussed in this element has been tried and tested and developed with R.A.I.D. and CTR High Risk Security Services Limited and can be purchased from both of them.

## Sprays
StoppaRed UV has been designed to be a UK legal self defence spray that anyone can carry. Ideal for anyone concerned with their personal safety, StoppaRed UV projects a thick and sticky stream onto the attacker. The formula is difficult to remove without water and the bright red colour helps you direct the stream accurately and to also identify the offender in the moments after the incident.

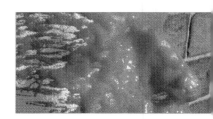

## Mobile Phones
Mobile phone technology has become so advanced that everyone is carrying one nowadays. The technology that can be utilised for security purposes is cost effective and reliable. With SOS Protect service you can have a contract mobile phone on any network and tariff. It allows you to activate a panic alarm which records 30 seconds of the call and provides the location to whom you choose to receive the panic.

## Tracking Device
Personal tracking devices have become more advanced and cost effective to use due to advancing technology. The ability of the new Sirf 3 GPS chip allows the device to work inside buildings and vehicles. The size of units has become smaller and it is now possible to design clothes and shoes and other items with built in tracking which is really good for child security. The mapping software is more advanced so that you have choices with regards to mapping and aerial photography.

## THINK POINT DETERRENCE 4

4.1 DEVELOP A PERSONAL PROTECTION PLAN FOR ONE OF THE FOLLOWING: HOME, STREET, VEHICLE, PUBLIC TRANSPORT, WORK OR PERSONAL PROTECTION EQUIPMENT.

SEE YOUR INSTRUCTOR FOR WORKSHEET (IF YOU ARE TAKING EXAM)

# DETECT

# R.A.I.D Defence Cycle / Rapid Action Initiated Defence

1 Confidence
2 Awareness
3 Conflict Management
4 Defence
5 Aftermath

RATIONAL THOUGHT

EMOTIONAL THOUGHT

## DETER

Develop more confidence, through learning Specialist Skills, which will create a Non Victim mentality and provide you with a safer way of living.

## DETECT

Through Awareness and visual Observation skills, you will be able to foresee potential situations before they arise by subtle indicators or triggers.

## DEFUSE

By following our S.T.O.P conflict management process, you will be able to de-escalate the situation, whilst preparing the mind and body to Escape or Defend.

## DEFEND

RAID Defence, works on the body's natural reflexes, which combined with universal defence concepts, make it easy to learn and remember when you need it most.

## DESENSITIZE

After a violent confrontation, you may suffer from denial or mental stress. We will provide the tools, techniques and advice to enable your recovery process.

PRE-ASSAULT (PRO-ACTIVE)

ASSAULT (RE-ACTIVE)

POST-ASSAULT (ACTIVE)

** This picture represents the processes of escalation from 1 to 5 of a physical confrontation unfolding

© 2008 to H2H Defence & CTR Services Ltd

# WELCOME TO DETECTION

**Founder/Chief Instructor**
Mr Tremaine Kent

Designed by Tremaine Kent, this module is the first module of reactive assault, in that you will have external confrontation stimulus. This is where you detect the potential of confrontation and attack and your emotions, heart and respiration rate increase. You will learn about the types of attacks and attackers so that you know how to recognise them. The best way we teach this is to place you in their shoes and get you to study how they choose their victims. You will learn observation skills which reinforces the previous module of deterrence awareness. The whole module culminates with the types of attacker delivery systems which are verbal and physical.

# AWARENESS & OBSERVATION

## "IF YOU HAVE KNOWLEDGE OF VIOLENCE AND YOU CAN IDENTIFY A POTENTIAL SITUATION THROUGH OBSERVATION, YOU STAND A BETTER CHANCE IN PREVENTING IT."

### What is Awareness?

Awareness is the knowledge of a subject that allows you to be conscious through observation. For example if you know about violence and confrontations and you understand the triggers and delivery systems attackers use, your consciousness will be able to react on subtle observations and allow you to avoid the potential situation. If you have no awareness, you probably will walk straight into a situation or place yourself within a situation without even knowing and be incapable of dealing with it.

Correct awareness of a situation could or will allow you to avoid it and that is the number one priority, as prevention is better than the cure. So how do you develop awareness? Well the first part is to gain the knowledge which you are doing by following this course. Then you should test your awareness in a sterile environment, by spending time being more observant of the environment you are in and by developing games in your training sessions. This leads us onto observation which feeds awareness.

### What is Observation?

Observation is the ability to see and hear things and interpret the information to make sense of it. Observation skills have been practiced and taught for many years to those that need to be able to use what they see on a daily basis, for example police officers are tested on observation skills and so are some units within the British Army. The mind is like a muscle in that if you train it, it will develop and grow. A professional author that deals with this subject is Tony Buzzens. He has discovered a way in which you can mind map what you see so that you can recall the information later. To elaborate on this, if you take the layout of your home for example, because you see it every day, it is subconsciously familiar to you. Then if you compartmentalise your home into areas such as front door and hall, kitchen, dining room, living room, stairs, toilet, master bedroom and so on, you have created areas you won't forget. His next rule is to involve all your senses such as taste, smell, feel, sight and sound when trying to remember something. Then it is as easy as making a story line. So lets say we had to remember a man that had attacked us or attacked someone else. You might start at your front door and imagine the man at your door. What does he look like? Does he remind you of someone that you can associate? Like a celebrity etc. What is he wearing? Well he has a striped shirt on with a fish tattoo on his neck so you could think the person that looks like someone I know is stood at my front door and has a stripey shirt like a deckchair at the seaside and he has a live wet fish attached to the chair which smells horrible. In this statement you have used three senses which are sight, touch and smell which allows you to compartmentalise that information.

So how is observation important in self defence and personal protection, well it has two distinct processes:

1. Prior assault and
2. Post assault.

### Prior assault

Prior assault is the ability to observe and identify potential situations before they arise; this is seeing things through a glimpse and negating or acting on what you have seen. There is a training aid to practice this which is called Kim's games. What you do is pick ten items and lay them on a table and cover them over with a towel, you then place yourself under physical pressure, like go for a run or do some exercises, and pull the towel off for 30 seconds then perform some more exercises for a little longer than before. Then you sit and write down all the items you saw and where they are on the table. This trains your brain to develop short term memory from sight under pressure.

### Post assault

Post assault of observation will be to record the whole event to be able to aid the police and services with the investigation if there is one.

# CONCLUSION

## "AWARENESS THROUGH KNOWLEDGE AND OBSERVATION CREATES AVOIDANCE"

Awareness and observation are at the foundation of our knowledge domain and combined are the most important factor in avoidance. If we understand what we see we can avoid or negate something well before we have to deal with a potential situation.

## THINK POINT DETECTION 1

**1.1 EXPLAIN THE TERMS OBSERVATION AND AWARENESS IN RELATION TO DETECTION WITHIN SELF DEFENCE AND CLARIFY THE DIFFERENCE BETWEEN THEM.**

SEE YOUR INSTRUCTOR FOR WORKSHEET (IF YOU ARE TAKING EXAM)

# AWARENESS & COLOUR CODING

## "AWARENESS AND ALERTNESS ARE A STATE OF MIND AND WITH OBSERVATION SHOULD BECOME A PART OF YOUR SUBCONSCIOUS."

### What is awareness through colour coding?

Colour coding is an awareness guide. The vast majority of people spend most of their lives unaware of their environments due to normal burdens that life places on them. Even job specific employment such as security and close protection work on shifts, so that the critical awareness

is at it's best for eight – twelve hours. Most victims are caught unaware and this module is designed to allow you to prioritize your awareness state of mind in relation to environmental or situational change.

The colour coding system R.A.I.D. employs is based on a colour representation of risk levels, and

so that it is easy to remember, R.A.I.D. has colour coded them in relation to the green cross code; as you know red is for stop or danger, amber or yellow is caution and green meaning go or safe. This also applies to stances and safety zones covered later.

**GO OR SAFE**

**CAUTION**

**STOP OR DANGER**

We will now look at each one in turn starting with the passive one first and moving up in severity.

# GREEN ZONE

- Safe Environment
- Enclosed Secure Area
- With Family or Friends
- Environment You Created

## Explanation

I want you to consider that you have had a hard day at work and on the way home you have been stuck in traffic or have been delayed and all you want to do is get home. When you walk in the door of your home you take a deep breath, throw your stuff down, walk into the living room, sit down and feel relaxed. The reason why so many of us do this, is that home is deemed our sanctuary which we have created ourselves and that subconsciously makes us feel safe and relaxed.

Coming home to family and friends where you feel relaxed and in your own domain is the green area or zone. If you have taken the necessary precautions when creating this environment with security in mind, your awareness is very low and your conscious thoughts on security and remaining alert start to move to the back of your mind.

# AMBER ZONE

- Outside Environment
- Daylight Hours
- Familiar Environment
- Around People

## Explanation

As soon as you leave home, the green zone or secure environment, you normally start to become everyday aware, which is awareness of where you are going to, how you are going to get there, if you need to take something with you or any environmental awareness that will allow you to function normally. With security in mind you should follow some form of personal security plan, this will enable you to negate 90% of none serious potential problems you may encounter.

The R.A.I.D. personal security plan has been designed and taught for many years to close protection, military and security related operatives and is recognised by the Bucks New University and the Security Industry Authority for licensing laws. The acronym S.A.F.E.R taught in the last module will provide a certain security plan.

# RED ZONE

- Outside Environment

- Night Time Hours

- Unfamiliar Environment

- Alone

### Explanation

Code red means you are focused and consciously considering what your senses tell you. If you are out of a safe zone and feel uneasy or there is a reason to be uncomfortable, you should be considering all possibilities due to the fact your sight and hearing are working harder to process information. It may also be a good time to consider "what if" scenarios and also constantly looking for potential safe zones.

For individuals that work within hostile environments this type of awareness becomes very tiring and a part of everyday life. If you know that you will be placing yourself in this environment or situation you can also take security precautions and carry personal attack alarms, spray, personal panic GSM alarms or locate devices mentioned in personal security equipment.

## THINK POINT DETECTION 2

**2.1 SUMMARISE THE COLOUR CODING ALERT SYSTEM**

SEE YOUR INSTRUCTOR FOR WORKSHEET (IF YOU ARE TAKING EXAM)

# TYPES OF ATTACKERS

## "TO KNOW YOUR ATTACKER IS TO KNOW THE ATTACK, TO KNOW THE ATTACK IS TO KNOW THE DEFENCE"

### Introduction to attackers

Obviously there are many forms of attack and to categorise all of them would be a huge subject, however we do appreciate one thing and that is the more you know about them the better your awareness will be so that you can avoid them.

There seems to be two different mindsets regarding such attacks as muggings, rape, assault and murder and they are the planned and opportunist attacks. We will look at both of these individually, before we place them under any attack type headings.

### Planned attack

These attacks are premeditated and are usually calculated against the risk of failure or consequence over victory and gains. The person that plans may be cold blooded, malicious and have a history of success or failures for their attacks. Due to the premeditation more often than not there will be no pre-assault phase and no dialogue. This is why we train the one to five principle covered later in the course.

### Opportunist attack

These attacks may suffer consequence and normally only attack if the environment and situation presents itself and favours them. Without your awareness and colour coding you can become an attractive prime target for the opportunist.

With both of these there has always been little to no regard to human life and in some cases the attacker may be overwhelmed or compelled to attack due to their own personal situation, background or history. We should not try to understand their reasons for attacking as there are professionals that are trained to deal with this; we are primarily concerned for our own safety and survival when confronted.

National statistics suggest that there is a reduction in one area of violence but really all that has happened is that it has been placed into a different category. With lenient sentences in prison, which is possibly due to overcrowding and the fact that some see prison as a badge of honour and prestige, not to mention that conditions have dramatically increased with human rights groups. This all affects the moral consequence of most attackers in that they are not worried about their aftermath of violent confrontation.

According to a new Home Office report, crime to individuals and households costs £36 billion a year and an increase has been seen in violent attacks by strangers on the streets of England. Many people try to equate our crime statistics to such countries as the USA and even Africa, however on both occasions if you compare the geographical land mass comparison we are the same if not worse for crime.

The categories that we follow are descendants of the categories and subcategories that the police and Home Office record. Such statistics are divided into the following areas:

# TYPES OF ATTACKERS

CATEGORIES

## 1. VIOLENCE AGAINST PERSONS (VAP)

### MOST SERIOUS (VAP)

VIOLENT OFFENCES WHERE THE INJURY INFLICTED OR INTENDED IS LIFE THREATENING AND OFFENCES RESULTING IN DEATH REGARDLESS OF INTENT

- MURDER
- MANSLAUGHTER
- HOMICIDE
- ATTEMPTED MURDER
- GRIEVOUS BODILY HARM (GBH)

### OTHER (VAP)

INCLUDES OFFENCES INVOLVING LESS SERIOUS WOUNDING OR INJURY. ALSO INCLUDES OFFENCES OF NO PHYSICAL INJURY BUT SERIOUS INTENT

- THREAT OR CONSPIRACY TO MURDER
- LESS SERIOUS WOUNDING
- ACTUAL BODILY HARM (ABH)
- ASSAULT WITHOUT INJURY (COMMON ASSAULT)

SUB CATEGORIES

| STRANGER (VIOLENCE) DANGER | ACQUAINTANCE (VIOLENCE) DANGER | MUGGING (VIOLENCE) DANGER | DOMESTIC (VIOLENCE) DANGER |

**COVERED LATER**

RAID CATEGORIES

**PHYSICAL ATTACKS**

**MUGGING ATTACKS**

**MEN**

# 2. SEXUAL OFFENCES (SO)

## MOST SERIOUS (SO)

THIS GROUP ENCOMPASSES RAPE, SEXUAL ASSAULT WHICH MAY INCORPORATE SERIOUS VIOLENCE AGAINST A PERSON

- RAPE – FEMALE +16
- RAPE – FEMALE - 16
- RAPE – FEMALE - 13
- RAPE – MALE +16 OR UNDER
- SEXUAL ASSAULT FEMALE
- INDECENT ASSAULT

## OTHER (SO)

THIS GROUP COVERS UNLAWFUL SEXUAL ACTIVITY WHICH ALSO MAY INCLUDE OTHER VIOLENCE AGAINST A PERSON

- ABDUCTION OF A FEMALE
- INDECENT EXPOSURE
- PROSTITUTION

CATEGORIES

**RAPE DANGER**

**ABDUCTION DANGER**

SUB CATEGORIES

**COVERED LATER**

**SEXUAL ATTACKS**

RAID CATEGORIES

**WOMEN**

# VIOLENCE AGAINST PERSONS

### Stranger Violence Danger

As the definition details this can be any form of attack from individuals under the influence of drink or drugs on a night out determined to cause trouble, road rage, and opportunist physical attacks at night. There are no parameters to where this form of attack may take place or the time of day and environment it may happen.

Only 27% of these attacks involve weapons and out of them 7% are bottles and 5% knives. 52% suffer no injuries and 32% minor injuries

**"CLASSIFIED AS ASSAULTS AND WOUNDING IN WHICH THE VICTIM DID NOT KNOW ANY OF THE OFFENDERS IN ANY WAY."**

### Acquaintance Violence Danger

As the definition details, this form of attack may derive from revenge, argument attacks or attacks between people that may know each other. Examples of this may be feuding neighbours, family disputes, rival gang or internal gang fighting, history related revenge attacks etc. Again there are no parameters to where this form of attack may take place or the time of day and environment it may happen.

The statistics are similar to the previous except 10% of weapons used are by hitting implements.

**"CLASSIFIED AS ASSAULTS AND WOUNDING IN WHICH THE VICTIM KNEW ONE OR MORE OF THE OFFENDERS, AT LEAST BY SIGHT."**

### Mugging Violence Danger

As the definition details this form of attack may be armed or unarmed depending on the type of attacker. If weapons are used they are normally done so to increase fear. Muggings can take many forms from the running snatching of bags by teenagers, cash point holdups to physical muggings by groups or individuals. Normally they happen in areas that the environment allows them to get what they want unless they are under the influence of drugs and alcohol.

The statistics lend themselves to majority non armed and 16% by knife point.

**"CLASSIFIED AS ROBBERY OR ATTEMPTED ROBBERY AND SNATCH THEFT FROM PERSON"**

### Domestic Violence Danger

Domestic violence is a large area and there are more non reported cases of this form of attack than the others. This form of attack is not limited to just women, it is men also that suffer from domestic violence. In some cases the powers that be have their hands tied dealing with these forms of attack and victims rely heavily on the aid agencies to provide counselling and advice. Most domestic violence cases happen in the home environment.

**"CLASSIFIED AS ASSAULTS AND WOUNDING WHICH INVOLVE PARTNERS, EX-PARTNERS OR OTHER RELATIVES"**

# SEXUAL OFFENCES

### Rape Danger

There are many forms of rape from date rape, matrimonial rape, drug rape, holiday rape and even male rape. The main point to consider is consent and how important it is to know that "No" means "No" irrespective of gender. Rape can occur within numerous environments and it depends on factors that will be discussed in more detail later. Information regarding statistics for all sexual offences are clouded by the fact that so many cases go unreported and organisations such as Rape Crisis have more calls for help to prove this. It is interesting to note that about 50% of rape victims don't report the crime.

**"CLASSIFIED AS AN ACT OF VIOLENCE AND DOMINATION AND ANGER. IT USES SEXUAL ACTS INCLUDING PENETRATION AS A WEAPON."**

### Abduction Danger

Abduction danger in its own context is not a common occurrence and the way we view this form of attack would be in relation to the 8% stranger rape attacks when a rapist would abduct you and then take you to the place they feel safe enough to rape you. Obviously with adults, for this to happen there would have to be a degree of force used and threats could be accompanied with the use of weapons for compliance tools. With regards to statistical data on this form of attack, there is no clear statistical information other than there has been a drop in recorded abductions of women from 2006 to 2007.

**"CLASSIFIED AS THE CRIMINAL TAKING AWAY A PERSON BY PERSUASION (CONVINCING SOMEONE – PARTICULARLY A MINOR OR A WOMAN HE/SHE IS BETTER OFF LEAVING WITH THE PERSUADER), BY FRAUD OR BY OPEN FORCE OR VIOLENCE."**

### Summary

To summarize the types of attackers and the national statistics we have highlighted a few main points as follows:

- THE RISK OF BEING A VICTIM OF VIOLENT CRIME WAS 3.6% AND OF WHICH 16 TO 24 YEAR OLD MEN WERE MORE AT RISK.
- SINGLE, UNEMPLOYED PEOPLE WERE 8.3 AND 9% MORE AT RISK OF VIOLENT CRIME.
- PEOPLE THAT VISITED A PUB MORE THAN 3 TIMES A WEEK WERE 6% MORE AT RISK OF VIOLENT CRIME.
- WOMEN ARE 77% MORE LIKELY TO SUFFER DOMESTIC VIOLENCE THAN MEN.
- MEN ARE 76% MORE LIKELY TO SUFFER STRANGER ATTACKS THAN WOMEN.
- MEN ARE 22% MORE LIKELY TO BE WOUNDED AFTER AN ATTACK THAN WOMEN.
- YOU ARE 56% MORE LIKELY TO BE MUGGED WITH A KNIFE THAN ANY OTHER WEAPON.

Now we have studied and analysed the two different attack categories and their sub-categories outlined by the police and Home Office, the next progression in understanding them in relation to what happens on the street, is to look at them from a broader approach of the R.A.I.D headed attacks, physical attacks, muggings and sexual attacks which are detailed in the forthcoming elements.

A note to point out is that some of the topics covered don't discriminate the genders but purely work to statistical and factual knowledge. We will not teach you how to survive a fire on a space craft if you will never be an astronaut!

# SEXUAL ATTACKS

## "ATTACKS BY INDIVIDUALS OR GROUPS TO DOMINATE AND PENETRATE TO CAUSE PHYSICAL HARM AND INJURY."

### Introduction to sexual attacks

When we say "sexual attacks" we are really referring to rape as we are considering the worst possible scenario that you may be dealing with. Even though people still see rape being committed on women, there is now statistical data on males being raped. This session will identify key types of rape, types of rapist and the delivery systems.

From the statistical information provided earlier the true figures of stranger rape with abduction only makes up 8% of the overall rapes. Too many self defence and martial arts systems focus on the Ted Bundy's of the world and the true fact is that you are more inclined to be raped by someone you know.

The R.A.I.D. concepts you will be taught later in the course, have been developed for the serial rapist scenarios that deal with date rape, marital rape and drug rape scenarios that you are more likely to be in.

### Types of rape

There are many types of rape nowadays and this element will provide you with a clearer picture of what the types are. Be under no illusion, just because it falls under a different category they all hold the same consequences and should also receive the same level of response in your defensive concept.

**Date rape:** the media has aided in the inaccurate naming of this new date rape which is not new; men have been raping known women for ages and well before they stuck another label to it. The meaning of date rape is by being raped by a known man, or someone you are having a date with, it is claimed that this is not as traumatic as being raped by a complete stranger. Like all relationships they are developed on trust and when the woman says "no" irrespective of the relationship, it means no. Consent is something that is negotiated on each and every occasion and not taken for granted.

**Drug rape:** everyone has heard of the drug rohypnol which has been said to be used in this form of rape. The drug rape label was again created by media, the real cause of drug rape is the rapist themselves; well before rohypnol, alcohol was given to get women drunk so that they couldn't remember what had happened. If drugs are used, depending on the drug, it may render you helpless physically to do anything or possibly impair you by a loss of memory.

**Holiday rape:** we presume holiday rape to mean that women get raped on holiday by foreign men, however in many cases the rape is by men of the same nationality. The misuse of

power by men is a global thing and if you look at women that travel in groups of twos or more overseas to relax and have fun, the nightlife and its associated exploits are a perpetrator's paradise.

**Marital rape:** marital rape of a woman by their husband when it is non-consensual became illegal in 1991. Before then it was considered that women consented to men once and for all time once married. A former special constable who raped his wife seven times over five days after she told him she was leaving him was jailed for ten years after he kept her shackled to a radiator. This case would be one of a kind as it is hard to get a prosecution nowadays.

**Male rape** Male rape is not a new phenomenon, it just has not been reported on and rape has always been a crime associated with women. However it does exist, especially with regards to children and paedophilia. There are no real statistics for male rape but the principles are the same as rape to women except in the nature of buggery and lack of consent. It also should be said that it is not a homosexual crime.

### Types of rapists

Now you understand the types of rape out there, we will now look at the rapists themselves. Using methods from the USA and the Federal Bureau of Investigations (FBI), the profiling of rapists seems to fall under distinct categories, which are:

### Power-assertive rapist:

The power assertive rapist is the type who will claim to have a weapon but will only use it to ensure the victim's co-operation. With 44% of all rapes falling under this category it is the most common of all forms of rape. Men that are athletic, have a "macho" image of themselves, are more often than not the type who commit date rapes. They typically meet their victim in a bar or nightclub. Instead of targeting a specific victim, they look for an opportunity to get a woman alone with them, perhaps with an offer of a ride home or an invitation back to their place. They may con their victim into trusting them or letting them into their home, perhaps by posing as a policeman or repairman. Approximately 44% of rapes are committed by power-assertive rapists. He is physically aggressive and will use the amount of force needed to control his victim, with degrading or obscene language, using a weapon, slapping or punching but they may not intend to kill their victims.

**GENERALLY, BEGGING AND CRYING DOESN'T WORK WITH THIS GUY. IF YOU'RE GOING TO RESIST, YOU'VE GOT TO BE SERIOUS. YOU'VE GOT TO SCREAM AND FIGHT HIM AS HARD AS YOU CAN TO GET AWAY.**

### Anger-retaliatory rapist:

Anger retaliation is different because the perpetrator is actually out to punish women. Often carrying hate towards women this type of perpetrator will often substantially injure victims to the point where they require medical intervention or hospitalization. Roughly 30% of rapes fall into this category. He feels animosity towards women and wants to punish and degrade them. Often he is a substance abuser. He is impulsive and has an explosive temper. He looks for an opportunity to commit the rape rather than for a specific victim. He attacks spontaneously and brutalizes the woman into submission. He will grab you from behind and drag you into the bushes. He will often beat you to near-unconsciousness before committing the rape. Any level of resistance may well enrage him and cause him to beat the hell out of you until he gets what he wants. He's not looking to kill you, but the beating could be fatal.

**YOU DO NOT WANT TO CHALLENGE OR ENRAGE THIS TYPE OF RAPIST**

You could try to escape. If you cannot get away or incapacitate the assailant, it's best to submit and try to limit the level of violence of the assault to the extent that you can.

### Power-reassurance rapist:

The power reassurance or opportunity rapist is one who takes advantage of an opportunity to commit a rape. This is done in conjunction with another crime such as burglary, robbery or kidnapping. He lacks the self-confidence and interpersonal skills to develop relationships with women. He is passive and non-athletic. He lives or works near his victim and "pre-selects" her by peeping or stalking. He typically breaks in to her home in the early hours of the morning and awakens her. He uses minimal force and will threaten her with a weapon, but usually does not have one. He fantasizes that he is his victim's lover so he may ask her to disrobe or to wear a negligee and he will kiss her and engage in foreplay. The power-reassurance type accounts for

21% of rapists. He is the least violent type of rapist, and does not intend to hurt or kill you. Among the different types of rapists, he is most likely to be dissuaded if you scream, cry, plead or fight." In general it is more probable that you can discourage a rapist who uses this approach.

### Anger-excitement rapist:

By far the most dangerous type of rapist is the anger excitement rapist. This perpetrator wants his victim to be hurt. Often victims are killed. Fortunately, only 5% of all rapists fall into this category. However, almost all murder/rapes take place at the hands of these criminals. A sadist, who derives sexual gratification from inflicting pain. He is typically charming and intelligent. The crime is premeditated and rehearsed methodically in his mind before it is attempted. His victims may or may not be strangers. He will tie, gag and blindfold them and torture them over a period of days, even recording his crimes in a diary, taking photographs or videotaping them. 5% of rapists fit this description. Of the four types he is the most criminally sophisticated and difficult to catch. Often he kills his victims, either to get rid of a witness or to gratify a psychosexual need.

# MUGGING ATTACKS

## "THE THREATENING AND SHOW OF FORCE TO TAKE VALUABLES FROM YOU."

### Introduction to mugging

From statistical information, the muggers we will be discussing are the ones that use force to take personal valuables from you. With many people living in the world of mobile phones and iPods, it is not surprising that we present a victim mentality from petty criminals to professional muggers. We are not coveted about our wealth and we tend to walk around in colour code green. From statistics it has been proven that the common weapon of choice is the knife or edged weapon as once displayed provides a high degree of fear and allows intimidated co-operation. There are signs and triggers that you can pick up on which increases your awareness so that you can avoid being a victim and this session will discuss these elements.

### Types of mugger

There are many types of mugger dependant on circumstances. We mentioned opportunists and planned attacks. This is not dissimilar to types of muggers as professional muggers tend to plan their attack and may work in groups, whereas an opportunist may see that you are putting valuables on offer and just run by and snatch the item without any communication or confrontation. The only other mugger is the desperate mugger who is clearly not worried by consequence or repercussions. To elaborate more on each of these types, here are some examples:

**Opportunist snatch mugger:** an individual who may be under the influence of drugs or alcohol, or may be dependant on them, who has to feed their habit and the only way to do this is by selling stolen items at ridiculous low prices that they get from unaware victims. For instances, women with open handbags showing their purse off, mobile phones at the ear, iPods, or any valuables on show that can be snatched in seconds. I have even heard of muggers on mountain bikes in London that snatch mobiles from passengers in cars that have the windows down who are stuck in traffic. If they see an easy target and can get away they will go for it.

**Planned professional mugger:** unlike the snatch and run mugger, this planned approach is the one that we are concerned with in that they calculate the risk and evaluate your suitability as a victim. They may probe their intended victim to evaluate the awareness levels and suitability. If they feel that you are too aware they will move onto their next victim. It is common for this type of mugging to involve more than one person as they will use diversionary tactics to move in. They will then pursue you to find the right environment to carry out their attack.

**Desperate mugger:** this potentially can be the worst form of mugging as the attacker is not worried about the consequences of their actions and if you have what they want they are taking it. If this form of mugger is threatening you with a weapon and the environment is not quiet, be cautious in your approach of handling the situation.

With all of these muggers there is no gender bias to who they will select as a victim. However if a man and woman with the same valuables were to become victims the woman would be more likely to be the victim. The main point to highlight is to keep your valuables covered up, don't show your wealth and remain aware as this will avoid victim selection.

## Body language of muggers

The body language of a mugger is dependant on what type they are and what kind of environment they are attacking you in, but here are a few signs and signals of common body language of muggers:

**Constant moving:** the mugger is constantly moving around you and violent probing of hands or head pecking. This will allow them to keep an eye on the surrounding environment if they are working alone.

**Erratic eye movements**: this accompanies the moving around as they are likely to be keeping an eye on you and the local area so that they don't get caught in the act.

**Concealed hands & side off position:** if they are always stood with a side away from you and their hand or hands are concealed then you need to be aware of the fact that they are potentially carrying a weapon. The reason the body is at a 45 degree angle is so that if they pull the knife, you get to see it and the body's natural instincts take over.

**Hand probing:** this may be a simple pat down or patting the chosen site of what they are after, for instance if they are going for your wallet they may tap the area of the pocket it is in and issue verbal commands.

**Nervousness:** unless they are professionals they may appear nervous and they may shake and appear pale. With today's CCTV and surveillance epidemic they may have a hoody on with their heads slightly lowered, or worst still wearing a ski mask.

## Delivery systems of muggers

Apart from the snatch and grab and the desperate muggers, the delivery systems are quite planned and complex in their nature. They develop into what seems a planned military operation from surveillance, evaluation to execution. Here is a typical delivery system for one lone mugger operating:

**Selection:** the victim is selected on a number of circumstances which are the awareness of the potential victim and if the valuables present themselves (worth doing). The mugger will try to identify more than one target and then study them.

**Surveillance**: once they have chosen their selected victim they will follow them and watch their every move, as well as keeping their eye on third party and environment. Once the victim has walked into an area that is isolated they make their first move.

**Physical probing**: once the mugger starts to move in the approach is more positive and they will ask the time or directions or some sort of question to get the feel of

the victim. If the victim is still unaware then this allows them to check around the area and pull out their hidden weapon. This is where their tone of voice and physical manner changes and they become dominant and aggressive. If the victim is aware then the mugger will still ask the question but then thank them and walk off.

**The attack:** once the attack has been initiated the knife or weapon will always be in view to them so that they know it is real, this will be accompanied with aggressive dialogue and large body postures. At this stage if it is taking too long or the victim is not complying 100% then a physical attitude adjustment will be given. This can be the blade pushed up against the neck or a punch to the face and head. Once they have what they want the mugger will flee the scene.

# PHYSICAL ATTACKS

## "ATTACKS BY INDIVIDUALS OR GROUPS TO VICTIMISE AND CAUSE PHYSICAL HARM AND INJURY."

### Introduction to physical attackers

As discussed earlier in the previous element, the stranger danger and acquaintance danger has been amalgamated into one category of physical attacks, so that you get a broader understanding of physical attacks which you potentially may encounter. From statistical information a man is 76% more likely to suffer this form of an attack than women and 16 – 24 year olds are more at risk, which is due to the fact that they are more socially active.

With the demands on the police, the extended drinking hours and the awareness of street crime and gang culture, I don't think that you can pick up a local newspaper without reading about an attack of some sort. This element is structured in a way that you can clearly understand the types, body language they use and the delivery indicators so that you can avoid them without physical confrontations.

**16 – 24 YEAR OLDS ARE MORE AT RISK, WHICH IS DUE TO THE FACT THAT THEY ARE MORE SOCIALLY ACTIVE**

### Types of attackers

There are many types of attacker on the street but the categories that R.A.I.D. has classified them under are "lone" and "group". The reason for this is that they fall under our initial anatomy of defence and the assumption rule covered later in the course.

To detail the motive of attack is impossible as there are too many variables and scenarios that you could imagine. We have outlined two main headings for you and annotated some simple examples.

**Lone attacker armed:** an individual who may be under the influence of drugs or alcohol, who is carrying a knife and who carries the knife because it makes him feel confident and power important. This individual is looking to find a victim that they can attack but will look for someone that they know they can beat with little resistance.

**Group attack armed:** a group or gang that may be local to an area that have to feel the need to have control over a particular area. The gang through successful intimidation gain confidence which, escalates to the use of weapons to dominate and terrorise the area.

**Lone attacker not armed:** an individual who you annoy by accident that feels that this is the last straw and confronts you, brings all the anger into the situation and wants to use you as a vessel to vent their frustration and pent up anger.

**Group attack not armed:** this may be a group out for a social night and you happen to be the victim of one of the group's attention. Because that

person is in a group you have the potential of friends joining in and sticking up for their friend.

As you can see, to actually describe every eventuality of type of attack would be ridiculous, this is why we provide the common key indicators so that you may understand as much about your potential attacker as you can prior to it becoming physical. The other point to make here is that it is vitally important to know if the attacker is armed or not as this may change the level of response you may legally use.

### Body language of attackers

The typical body language of a person that wants a physical confrontation with you has certain traits, which are a physiological means of preparing their own body for action. These signs or signals are good indicators which you may well pick up on:

### Side ways moving
This is a physiological way of appearing larger than life and it may range from shifting body weight to actually pacing side to side.

### Arms open and beckoning
This is another means of making their body larger than life and in this position the arms and guard are down and to the sides, which is a good point to note from a defensive point of view.

### Focused eyes
The eyes of your attacker will be wide and fixed as the adrenaline races through their veins and accelerates the body.

### Erratic hand movements
The hands will be moving erratically and physical gestures, will be signalled.

### Delivery systems of attackers
With physical attacks, there normally is a chain of progression to violence depending on the proximity or environment. The delivery system is how the attacker actually gets from a position of distance to a position of striking you physically and by mentally building them up, some call this the pressure cooker effect.

To understand the delivery system and how the visual, verbal and physical methods work, we shall look at them in turn:

### WITH PHYSICAL ATTACKS, THERE NORMALLY IS A CHAIN OF PROGRESSION OF VIOLENCE

### Visual
The visual delivery system is normally the longest distance in that you may be in a crowded room and you get that feeling someone is staring at you; when you turn to look, you notice that someone is staring at you. This is not a normal stare but a piercing one with intent. Your reaction to this should be one of confidence but not irritation and look away ensuring that you have made them aware that you know they are there. This should then be the disengagement point of the situation.

### Verbal
When the visual has not allowed escalation or the proximity has changed, the verbal delivery depending on the motive, will be the next escalation and allow the attacker to feel you out. What I mean by this is a means to see your response to dialogue, which normally is profound and graphic such as "What are you looking at?", "Do you want a fu\*\*ing picture?" to "Do you want a go you prick?". These are all used to see if you will take it to the next level by the dialogue you use in response. Here is an example of two verbal deliveries and the responses given, the scene is a public club at night stood at the bar:

1. ATTACKER SAYS, "OI YOU FU\*\*ER, WHAT ARE YOU LOOKING AT?"

   VICTIM RESPONDS, "YOU, YOU PRICK, WHY?"

2. ATTACKER SAYS, "OI YOU FU\*\*ER, WHAT ARE YOU LOOKING AT?"

   VICTIM RESPONDS, " I'M WAITING FOR MY GIRLFRIEND, SHE WENT TO THE TOILET AND I AM LOOKING FOR HER!"

In these two examples it is easy to see which one escalates the situation, as a negative response breeds escalation which can be what the attacker is looking for. Sometimes they need a reason to go physical and what you say can help them achieve this. Another thought to add to this is the tone of voice used and the way they say it, whether it is loud, aggressive etc, you should try to remain confident so that the situation doesn't go the other way and the attacker sees you as a weak victim.

### Physical
The physical would be the next delivery after they have verbally assaulted you or it might be physical straight away, this depends a lot on proximity and environment. This is not to be confused with the attack, as it is still a means to evaluate your response and to give them the

reason to have a fight. The common physical deliveries are:

**Finger pointing**: poking the finger in the chest and sometimes in your face, which can be annoying if you haven't experienced it.

**Shoving one**: or two handed, this you all must have seen one time or another. Even school children know how to do this as they use it a lot in the playground. Both of these involve a high placement of hands to the top half of your body, which can be potentially dangerous as you may get sucker punched and not be able to stop it. If the attacker feels that you are too strong for them, what I mean by this is that if they shove you and you respond submissively, they know they are stronger and their body language grows, with their arms and guard coming down and chest puffing up. Whereas if you respond with an aggressive posture and dig your heels in, the attacker's guard goes up and they prepare to fight or possibly back down.

**Bump or knock**: this type of delivery can be non-committal as it gives them the option to bail out of the escalation. This means if they bump into you they are giving you the option to respond and in some circumstances they are bumping to annoy or irritate you

to become aggressive so that the escalation is created and physical violence is instigated. As with most of the subjects we have covered thus far, avoidance is the key and the way to deal with this is to keep moving in the direction you are going to create distance and acknowledge the knock by apologising. This way the only escalation the attacker has is to follow you, which shows you their intent.

# NOTES (PLEASE USE THIS AREA FOR NOTES)

## THINK POINT DETECTION 3

**3.1   DRAW CONCLUSIONS ABOUT THE TYPES OF ATTACKERS YOU DEEM AS BEING YOUR MAIN THREAT AND THE WAYS THEY OPERATE.**

SEE YOUR INSTRUCTOR FOR WORKSHEET (IF YOU ARE TAKING EXAM)

# DEFUSE

# R.A.I.D Defence Cycle / Rapid Action Initiated Defence

**1** Confidence  **2** Awareness  **3** Conflict Management  **4** Defence  **5** Aftermath

RATIONAL THOUGHT

EMOTIONAL THOUGHT

## DETER

Develop more confidence, through learning Specialist Skills, which will create a Non Victim mentality and provide you with a safer way of living.

## DETECT

Through Awareness and visual Observation skills, you will be able to foresee potential situations before they arise by subtle indicators or triggers.

## DEFUSE

By following our S.T.O.P conflict management process, you will be able to de-escalate the situation, whilst preparing the mind and body to Escape or Defend.

## DEFEND

RAID Defence, works on the body's natural reflexes, which combined with universal defence concepts, make it easy to learn and remember when you need it most.

## DESENSITIZE

After a violent confrontation, you may suffer from denial or mental stress. We will provide the tools, techniques and advice to enable your recovery process.

PRE-ASSAULT (PRO-ACTIVE)

ASSAULT (RE-ACTIVE)

POST-ASSAULT (ACTIVE)

** This picture represents the processes of escalation from 1 to 5 of a physical confrontation unfolding

© 2008 to H2H Defence & CTR Services Ltd

# WELCOME TO DEFUSE

**Founder/Chief Instructor**
Mr Tremaine Kent

Designed by Tremaine Kent, this is the second part of the escalation after you have detected the confrontation and you are not able to get away. By now you will be feeling the effects of emotional adrenaline and physiological change, like accelerated heart and respiration rate, dry mouth etc. This module is important and overlooked in traditional martial arts because it provides a study of the laws relating to self defence and also provides the Means, Opportuntiy and Intent (MOI)

use of force ladder and tactical system called the "S.T.O.P. emergency directive", which takes you through conflict management, active listening and de-escalation skills needed to enable the reintroduction of rational thought processing. The module finishes on deflection skills, by verbal and physical means and teaches you the way to pattern interrupt the attacker, which may be your last attempt to get away before the situation turns physical.

# THE LAW

## "DON'T BECOME A VICTIM OF THE COURTS WHEN YOU HAVE PROTECTED YOURSELF ON THE STREET."

### Introduction to the law

Before you consider any legal ramifications of any actions you make to defend yourself on the street, it is important to consider the legal consequence as a strategic proactive consideration and not one while you are in the midst of a confrontation as this will lead to hesitation and probably getting hurt. However, unless you know your rights and know the law pertaining to them, you could place yourself in jail just by saying the wrong things. Even when individuals have defended themselves within the law, in their statements to the police and subsequent court appearance they have been prosecuted for a technicality of what they said and not on what they did or what happened.

I remember a student that was confronted by a group of guys, five to be exact after a night out, he said that he tried to de-escalate the situation and look for an exit point but one of the guys became more aggressive and moved in on him. Now consider this: If he was attacked he would most probably be in a world of pain. So he pre-empted any attack and palmed the guy in the face and made his exit at speed. Did he commit a crime? Well it depends on how you look at it and what you would say. Here are two examples from this scenario:

1. I THOUGHT HE WAS GOING TO ATTACK SO I THOUGHT I'D GET THE FIRST ONE IN AND SMASHED HIM IN THE FACE.

2. HE LUNGED AT ME AND I INSTINCTIVELY BROUGHT MY ARM UP TO DEFEND MYSELF. I PUSHED HIM AWAY AS I HAD THE HONEST BELIEF THAT THEY WERE GOING TO ATTACK ME AND THAT MY LIFE WAS IN DANGER. BY PUSHING HIM AWAY I USED ENOUGH REASONABLE FORCE AS TO MAKE MY ESCAPE FROM THE VOLATILE SITUATION THEY PLACED ME IN.

By these two examples you can see how one sounds more aggressive than the other and that in the second example the crucial parts are "I had an honest belief" and "reasonable force". So even after a confrontation the defence process is still ongoing and you need to be able to defend yourself from possible prosecution.

As well as the fore mentioned, when or if you go to court, there are other factors that will be considered. For example if you were regularly attending traditional arts classes but the system you were learning was, for example, called combat karate, the mere word of combat lends itself to misinterpretation and can be associated with aggression, warfare, attack etc. So even though you attend the classes for personal protection, a court may see this as you are trained to attack and cause harm which may affect your defence. This is why Rapid Action Initiated Defence is an acronym and no mention to combat even the H2H defence is passive, not to mention the process of the five D's and how they work on avoidance and de-escalation strategies.

Many martial arts systems do not teach the legal aspects of defence as they have no reason to as they are based on technical sporting applications. This can be potentially dangerous on the street as the commensurate level of force and the way it is delivered will not match the aggression being shown and will place you outside of the law.

The two main laws we will be considering during this session are:

1. The criminal law act 1967

2. The human rights act 1998

Both of which pertain to personal defence and the amount and use of force used within defence.

## Criminal Law Act 1967

The Criminal law Act governs behaviour that breaks the rules of society. As an act of parliament, it therefore has to be investigated by the police and prosecutions are conducted by the crown prosecutions service, if they have enough evidence. The evidence against must prove beyond reasonable doubt that you are guilty. The act states:

**A PERSON MAY USE FORCE AS IS REASONABLE IN THE CIRCUMSTANCES IN THE PREVENTION OF CRIMES**

In layman's terms it means a person must be able to justify their actions in court and prove their actions were reasonable in the circumstances with the level of force shown. The circumstances behind the situation will also be brought to bare. Force may only be used under the following:

- Reasonable in the circumstances.

- An absolute necessity.

- The minimum amount necessary.

- Proportionate to the seriousness of the case.

Furthermore a person about to be attacked does not have to wait for his/her assailant to strike the first blow, circumstances may justify a pre-emptive strike. To give

you an example of reasonable force, if you were confronted by an attacker and he grabbed you, you should match the force reasonably enough to make your escape. If you took him to the ground and repeatedly kicked him in the head, this would be deemed unreasonable and excessive force.

## Human Rights Act 1998

Under the human rights act, everyone is entitled to the right to life and the convention raises related issues in respect of proportionality.

- Is the force used proportionate to the wrong that it seeks to avoid or the harm it seeks to prevent?

- Is the use of force chosen the least intrusive or damaging practicable option?

So the proportionality is the key word and in layman's terms it means the minimum amount that matches the force against you. So if an attacker grabbed you, you would not be lawful to stab him with a knife as this is not proportionate.

Both of these laws are very vague and can mean anything. With this total ambiguity you have to make some move towards what will be acceptable and lawful without relying on open ended meanings.

So the first consideration to the law that you will look at is what are you confronted by, and some

ground rules for classification. The way you do this is by seeing the attacker through the eyes of his defence lawyer. You need to prove without doubt that you were lawful in using self defence and the particular amount of force.

# THE LEGAL TRIANGLE

The defence lawyer for the attacker will try to use everything within his power to discredit you and show that you had alternative options available. I remember a friend being requested for jury service, the case they had was a young man that was threatened by another man wielding a knife. The young man defended himself and in the process punched the knife attacker in the face. During the court appearance it became knowledge that the young man was an exceptional boxer, due to this he was prosecuted for damages to the knife attacker because he was trained to cause harm through punching and should have had more self control... well can you imagine what my friend said... This is what you are up against and the lawyers will bend the law to get their clients off.

So to understand when to use self defence we have developed the legal triangle which is your red or green light to act or not.

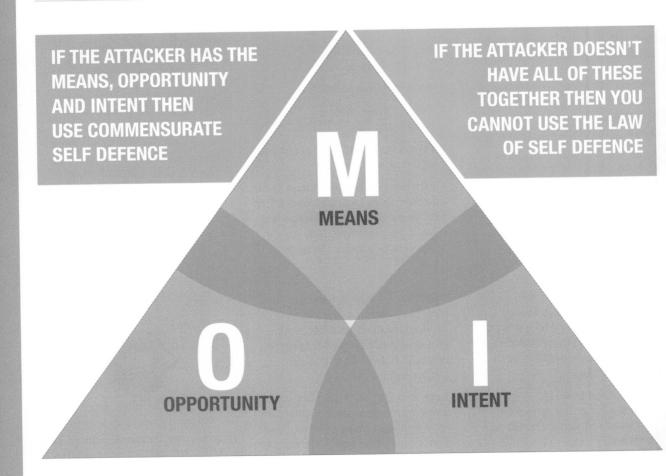

IF THE ATTACKER HAS THE MEANS, OPPORTUNITY AND INTENT THEN USE COMMENSURATE SELF DEFENCE

IF THE ATTACKER DOESN'T HAVE ALL OF THESE TOGETHER THEN YOU CANNOT USE THE LAW OF SELF DEFENCE

**M**
MEANS

**O**
OPPORTUNITY

**I**
INTENT

**MEANS:** THE ATTACKER HAS A WEAPON OR IS PHYSICALLY ABLE TO CAUSE HARM.
**OPPORTUNITY:** THE ATTACKER IS WITHIN DISTANCE TO CAUSE HARM OR YOUR EXIT IS BLOCKED.
**INTENT:** THE ATTACKER SHOWS BY PHYSICAL OR VERBAL MEANS THAT THEY ARE GOING TO CAUSE HARM.

# R.A.I.D USE OF FORCE LADDER

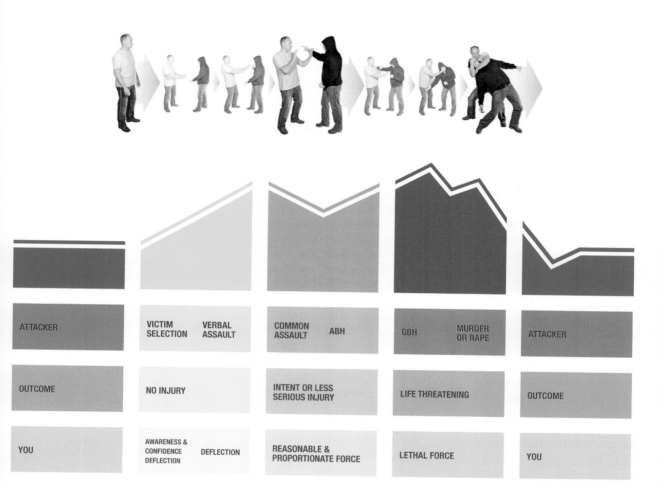

| ATTACKER | VICTIM SELECTION | VERBAL ASSAULT | COMMON ASSAULT | ABH | GBH | MURDER OR RAPE | ATTACKER |
|---|---|---|---|---|---|---|---|
| OUTCOME | NO INJURY | | INTENT OR LESS SERIOUS INJURY | | LIFE THREATENING | | OUTCOME |
| YOU | AWARENESS & CONFIDENCE DEFLECTION | DEFLECTION | REASONABLE & PROPORTIONATE FORCE | | LETHAL FORCE | | YOU |

## THINK POINT DEFUSE 1

1.1 CLARIFY THE CRIMINAL LAW ACT AND THE HUMAN RIGHTS ACT IN RELATION TO SELF DEFENCE.
1.2 EXPLAIN THE R.A.I.D. (RAPID ACTION INITIATED DEFENCE) USE OF FORCE LADDER.

SEE YOUR INSTRUCTOR FOR WORKSHEET (IF YOU ARE TAKING EXAM)

# CONFLICT MANAGEMENT SYSTEM

## "A PROCESS OF MANAGING CONFLICT AND ALLOWING YOU OPTIONS. IF AN ATTACKER CAN BE MADE TO TALK — THEY MAY LET YOU WALK."

### Introduction

Through previous modules we have discussed Deterrence, which is the way we create the non victim mentality through confidence, and Detection which provides the understanding of potential situations and attacker methodologies. This session will look at conflict management and how you can cope with a potential attack if you have been unable to avoid one. Now that you are dealing with a greater potential of physical attack you have to try and de-escalate or defuse the situation to allow you the potential of exit or prepare for any attack stimulus. Self defence is not just about the physical defence, in fact it is more of 60% psychological, 25% emotional and only 15% physical. With this in mind we have created a dynamic directive which roughly translates as an on the move execution of an order, which in this case is the acronym S.T.O.P.

**SELF DEFENCE IS:**
**60% PSYCHOLOGICAL**
**25% EMOTIONAL**
**15% PHYSICAL**

So imagine that you have not been able to avoid a situation and you are confronted by an attacker? What do you do? What do you say? How do you react? Well all of these questions within traditional arts and systems would have you attack or defend as they put it. I remember a guy at a tube station in London asking me for directions, but he was stood side onto me which I found strange and he had one arm behind his back. At that time the S.T.O.P. directive was already in my mind and whilst providing directions my nearest hand was hovering around the arm behind his back covering it. All of a sudden he pulled something from his back pocket and I blocked his arm, only to find out that it was a network map of the stations. Now considering the time and environment I was right to be cautious so after seeing what it really was I apologised, he responded "no problem" and went on his way. The point to this story is that in most systems if you feel vulnerable and you have no conflict management training your auto response in this situation is either to freeze or attack because there is a knowledge void. By using the S.T.O.P. dynamic directive you will be able to pilot yourself through the situation whilst remaining a lot safer and prepared for any stimulus.

### So what is the S.T.O.P. emergency directive?

No matter if someone is shoving you, shouting at you, or if you feel that something is wrong and you detect a potential attack is about to happen, the S.T.O.P. directive will place you physically and emotionally in a position of safety, to allow you the ability to cope with the situation. To explain this in more detail we have designed a diagram which outlines the whole process and shows you the escalation direction with each directive in turn as a scenario unfolds. Before you read any further, obviously this will seem to be a lot to learn and take on board, however you will instinctively go through these processes and guides without thought as the training will make it come naturally

### THE STOP DIRECTIVE WILL PLACE YOU PHYSICALLY AND EMOTIONALLY IN A POSITION OF SAFETY

Please note that you may be able to exit and escape further escalation at any stage and this will be your optimal directive as is to avoid a situation.

# R.A.I.D STOP EMERGENCY DIRECTIVE

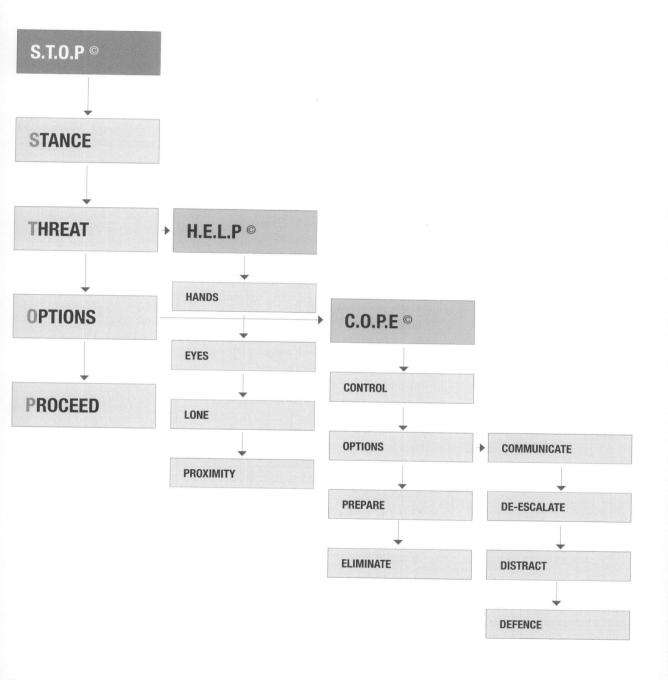

**S.T.O.P** ©

**S**TANCE

**T**HREAT → **H.E.L.P** ©

**O**PTIONS

**P**ROCEED

HANDS

EYES

LONE

PROXIMITY

**C.O.P.E** ©

CONTROL

OPTIONS → COMMUNICATE

PREPARE → DE-ESCALATE

ELIMINATE → DISTRACT

DEFENCE

THIS WHOLE PROCESS MAY TAKE SECONDS FROM START TO FINISH OR MAY BE PROTRACTED DEPENDING ON THE SITUATION, BEAR IN MIND THAT MOST STREET FIGHTS CAN BE AS SHORT AS 30 SECONDS LONG.

# STANCE

**"A GREAT FIGHTER (DEFENDER) MAKES HIS EVERYDAY STANCE HIS FIGHTING (DEFENDING) STANCE AND HIS FIGHTING (DEFENDING) STANCE HIS EVERYDAY STANCE" MUSASHI**

| S.T.O.P © |
| :--- |
| **STANCE** |
| THREAT |
| OPTIONS |
| PROCEED |

## Introduction

When confronted, the body language you present is vitally important and should not display any signs of aggression or confrontation and also be in the best position to be able to react effectively and responsively.
To give you added safety you need to be able to conceal your true intentions and as 60% of communication is body language, you need to have the skills necessary to be able to override your emotions and adopt a safe, non aggressive stance.

There are three types of stance we teach in R.A.I.D. which are similar to many other systems, and they are, the natural stance (your everyday normal rational stance or everyday positions such as sitting, standing, leaning etc), the reactive stance (the initial de escalation submissive stance, when you are confronted by an attacker) and the active stance (when you are in the midst of defending yourself). There are no rules as to which one of these stances you must place yourself in, however the situation will normally dictate the stance you adopt.

Before we look at each in turn, a point to make is that in some situations you may want to step backwards to create distance between you and the attacker, this is not always the best thing to do as you are unaware of what is behind you, so try to move sideways and preferably away from their leading tool and towards an exit point to escape.

## Natural stance

When we say natural stance, we don't mean a particular stance or posture, but actually your day to day, moment to moment positions of your body. No matter what you are doing you must be able to defend yourself without the opportunity to get into a preferred stance or posture. Awareness to a potential situation will normally take you out of a natural stance and move you into a reactive or active stance depending on the speed of escalation.

## Reactive stance

As the title suggests, this stance is reactive to stimulus. When you are confronted the reflexive response is to naturally bring the hands up to chest height with open palms, which is the body's way of protecting your personal space. Not just with confrontations, this position is the body's reflexive defence system which will be adopted in most situations, some call it the fence, passive or submissive stance.

This is similar to when you are on the ground, your reflexive response kicks in and you adopt an almost foetal position with the arms and knees coming up to protect your body's core.

When you feel threatened the hands form a protective barrier at the edge of our personal space. To look at personal space in more detail, there are three personal space safety zones that you should consider which are:

### Personal space (defence area)
This is the RED area which you class as personal and normally only people that you trust are allowed to enter this area such as loved ones and good friends.

### Meeting space (defuse and de-escalation area)
This AMBER area is the distance that you would leave if you are meeting someone, others call this the postman distance as it needs to be close enough to make physical contact but not close enough to invade your personal space.

### Stranger space (awareness and observation area)
This GREEN area is the outer area your awareness is most heightened to, as it forms your outer defences. You can communicate at this distance without physical contact effectively.

The reactive stance is the most strategic stance the body can adopt in a confrontation and it provides you the maximum protection of your centre line whilst giving you the use of all your tools. So any attack made to the chest, neck or head will instinctively be cut short and stopped, without rational thought being necessary, as the reflexive response will not telegraph your intentions and react 100 times faster than any technically taught block.

The fundamental point of this stance is that you look submissive and with correct dialogue you make the attacker believe you are weaker. This doesn't escalate the situation and leads the attacker into a false sense of security, which lowers their guard and promotes their egos. This in turn draws them into your close quarter's tools.

### Active stance
This would commonly be known as the fighting stance. However the fundamental point with this stance is to create a stable moveable platform that allows you the responsive use of all your offensive tools with the ability to spontaneously react to attacker's movements and stimulus. Due to the fact that you are now in defence mode there is no need to cover your intentions and make them believe you are weaker. Quite the opposite, as it will now help to become larger than life and more aggressive. The principle of non-telegraphing your intentions still applies. So unlike the reactive stance the only change is your foot position, balance and hands in that weight is distributed evenly over a widened stance, which provides the stable balanced platform and hands turn from open handed palm showing to closed and palms facing inwards.

# RAID NATURAL, REACTIVE AND ACTIVE STANCE

## NATURAL
**(NORMAL EVERYDAY STANCE)**

## REACTIVE
**(INSTINCTIVE, RESPONSIVE STANCE)**

## ACTIVE
**(PROTECTIVE, RESPONSE STANCE)**

# THREAT

## "TO KNOW YOUR THREAT, IS TO KNOW HOW TO MINIMISE THE THREAT"

| S.T.O.P © | |
|---|---|
| **S**TANCE | |
| **T**HREAT | (H.E.L.P) |
| | **H**ANDS |
| | **E**YES |
| | **L**ONE |
| | **P**ROXIMITY |
| **O**PTIONS | |
| **P**ROCEED | |

### Introduction

Now you have adopted a reactive stance, your mind starts to compute what you are dealing with and assess the threat. H.E.L.P is another acronym tool that enables a fast means of quickly identifying the main areas of threat; this modified system has been used by the military for many years and to some extent allows you to minimise many assumptions. By using this tool you will be able to see the physical threats a potential attacker has and confirm them with any verbal threats used.

The H.E.L.P. tool considers the physical aspects of an attacker and stands for:

**H** FOR HANDS OF THE ATTACKER

**E** FOR EYES

**L** FOR LONE, IF ATTACKER IS WORKING ALONE OR IN A GROUP

**P** FOR PROXIMITY TO ATTACKER AND ENVIRONMENT

### H – Hands

When looking at the hands check to see if they are closed, open or hidden. Even hands that are in view can still conceal a weapon such as knives or edged implements. Also consider jewellery that they are wearing such as rings as these can still be dangerous on impact. If hands are concealed then move to the side furthest away and change your stance slightly to guard that area.

### E – Eyes

People's eyes are amazing for showing intent, there is scientific data on how the eyes reveal truth or lies and whether you are imagining or retrieving fact just by the way your eyes move. The main consideration with the eyes of an attacker is whether they are erratic and that they look to areas you should be aware of, for instance if an attacker has an accomplice then they may give you a sign of this through their eyes by quick glances at them. The eyes may also give you an understanding of where they might strike first but this is normally just before they do.

## L – Lone

This may come to you too late as a lot of people often comment after an attack that they didn't see it coming from the side by one of the attacker's mates. The idea of making a conscious effort to see if the attacker is on their own or in a group is vital as it will change the strategy you adopt to deal with multiple attackers. You may also look at your environment at the same time to see exit points. This also falls under our assumption rule which you always think the attacker is:

- ALWAYS ARMED
- ALWAYS WITH SOMEONE

## P – Proximity

The last part in assessing the threat is the proximity from you to the attacker or attackers and the environment, for instance are there objects around you that may aid or hinder you or are there exits where you can make your escape. The main point of this heading is to remain in control of the proximity so that you control the situation and environment you are in.

## THINK POINT DEFUSE 3

**3.1 EXPLAIN THE FOUR STEPS OF THE DYNAMIC THREAT ASSESSMENT (H.E.L.P.) WITHIN THE CONFLICT MANAGEMENT PROCESS.**

SEE YOUR INSTRUCTOR FOR WORKSHEET (IF YOU ARE TAKING EXAM)

# OPTIONS

## "IF YOUR ATTACKER CAN BE MADE TO TALK, YOU MAY BE ABLE TO WALK"

| S.T.O.P © | |
|---|---|
| STANCE | |
| THREAT | |
| **OPTIONS** | **(C.O.P.E)** |
| | CONTROL |
| | OPTIONS |
| | PREPARE |
| | ELIMINATE |
| PROCEED | |

### Introduction

By adopting the correct stance and assessing the threat you should be able to make your defence tactic fit the situation. To cope with this we have created the C.O.P.E tool which again guides you through the process to enable you a safe appropriate response. As we said previously if you haven't been able to exit the situation, C.O.P.E. allows you to create options of choice, which all happens within seconds of the confrontation. This unique tool is the heart of the conflict management process because it considers four main elements such as communication, de-escalation, distraction and defence, albeit we will discuss the defence systems in the next module. The communication you use can change the outcome of the potentially volatile situation and provide you time to choose the correct options to take. So the C.O.P.E. tool guides you through the natural progression of a situation and stands for:

**Control** Yourself and your environment

**Options** Create options through the following:

| | |
|---|---|
| 1. Communication | What blocks communication and how to effectively communicate with an attacker |
| 2. De-escalation | How to de-escalate by removing triggers and finding inhibitors |
| 3. Distraction | By using verbal and physical distractions you may be able to create time for greater options |
| 4. Defence | This module will be covered later |

**Prepare** Yourself mentally and physically

**Eliminate** Eliminate FEAR by visualization

### C – Control

In the fear management session of deterrence we looked at how fear is an emotion and that knowledge dispels fear. Well by now you are sure to be dealing with primary assault fear, so the first part of control is to control yourself and calm yourself down. You may have seen films or even been in a position when someone is becoming scared and erratic, another person may say "pull yourself together" and "snap out of it" whilst slapping their face.

Well this is because they are out of their comfort zone and due to fear they lose control of their emotions and turn their focus inwards of themselves. To combat this from happening there are numerous ways to deal with this, from focusing on the external and the situation to reliving a mental blueprint of a similar situation that had a good result. The main point to make is the more times you are placed into a scenario replication in training the more equipped you will be in a real confrontation.

In warfare the term "dominate the high ground" means that by dominating the environment you have a better chance of survival because strategically and tactically you are using the ground to your advantage. The same principle applies with you controlling your environment. You may use objects as barriers, or consider moving towards your final exit point. Look at as much of the environment as you can as you never know how the situation may change.

## O – Options

The options you have can lead you in many directions whether internal or external, for instance internally you are governed by the amount of knowledge you have of a particular situation, the more knowledge you have of the situation the more options you can choose, that's why mental blue printing in training through progressive scenario replication is so important.

Before we discuss options, the following escalation ladder outlines the extent of what is involved in creating options and coincides beautifully with the law that surrounds defence.

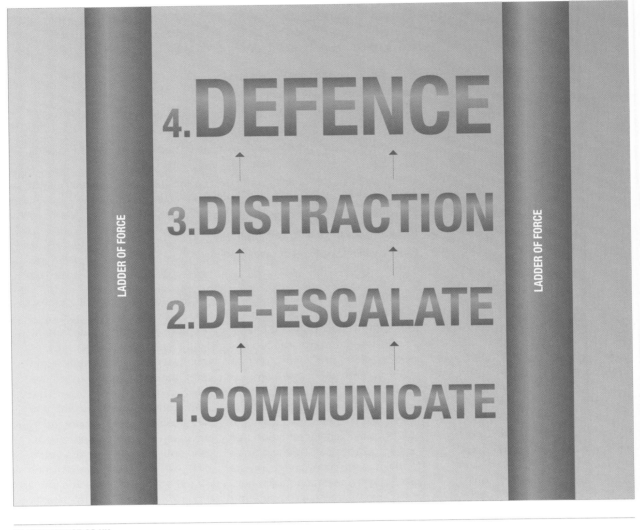

## 1. Communication

Communication is made up of 60% body language, 20% tone of voice and only 10% of actual words spoken in a confrontation. We have already considered body language in stance of STOP which suggests the correct stance to adopt to calm the situation down but still remain protected (reactive stance), now we must consider the verbal side of communication with tone and what is actually said. But before we do this, we will explain the communication path and how information is passed from one to another in a confrontation, detailed below:

 ← CHECK UNDERSTANDING →

| SENDER | | RECEIVER |
| --- | --- | --- |
| ENCODES | ▸ MESSAGE | ▸ DECODES |

Before the information is sent it will be affected by internal blocks then passed, during which time external blocks affect the message and then it is received. To become complete the message has to be checked or confirmed and depending on the internal and external blocks depends on what information is received. An example of an internal block may be alcohol as you know what to say but the words don't quite come out, and external blocks may be noise, a busy bar is making it hard to hear what is said. So here are a few common blocks to communication:

### INTERNAL

**Ego: emotional words used as opposed to common sense**

**Drugs and alcohol: affect brain processes and speech and thoughts are defused**

**Language: people with accents or even different languages**

### EXTERNAL

**Noise: environmental noise maybe loud**

**Groups: too many people talking at same time within the confrontation**

**Visual distractions: between or around the communication may affect concentration and active listening**

So to overcome this problem you should use active listening which is the way you use your body to move in acceptance or disagreement with what's being said (small nods or shaking head) and clear voice communications without shouting and inflating the situation. You should try to confirm their intentions so that you are clear on what they are doing and so that any possible witnesses can hear them (obviously in some attacks such as muggers or rapists this will not apply) and also bide your time.

The way you respond and the tone used should not be over them, but in fact be level with the view to slowly bringing the tone down, so they match it. If you do speak louder and harsher with them they will get louder and more aggressive. The words you respond with should also not escalate the situation even though what you say is only 10% of communication, however you can use what you say to your advantage as the attacker may be pushing you into a verbal negative response to fuel his anger to the next level.

Pattern interruption is the way of changing the attacker's focus through speech and questioning. The brain can only think of one thing at a time and two separate thoughts cannot exist at the same time. So you may use questions or sentences to pull them off their original chain of thought. An example of this is:

Attacker – "What the fu** you lookin at?", with this the attacker is looking for a negative response to take him to the next level and go physical. Those negative comments may be "I'm not" which will lead to you calling him

a liar or "I'm sorry" which leads to something like "Do you wanna picture?" and the list goes on.

To pattern interrupt Defender – "It's Paul isn't it, from school?", now the attacker is thinking and as we said the brain cannot have two thoughts existing at the same time, does he know this guy and why is he calling me Paul.

At this stage pattern interruption has occurred which can lead you to a number of options.

## 2. De-escalation
Before we discuss de-escalation we will look at the escalation process and what actually triggers a situation to increase. Unlike other conflict management programs and systems, you need to start from an initial confrontation as self defence is about survival and the possibilities of a violent confrontation. Here is an escalation ladder to explain how an initial confrontation turns into a violent situation.

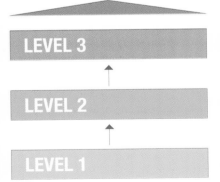

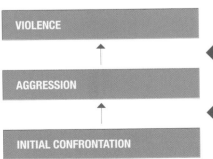

From the initial confrontation, the body language you present and tone of voice can trigger aggression which fuels the attackers reason to become physical. From aggression once it has risen to a certain stage (which can be noticed through the session on types of attackers in detection module) the sharp outburst of violence will be initiated. With all triggers there are inhibitors, however they depend on the type of attacker you are dealing with.

### TRIGGERS

**Body language: the way you stand and the posture you present may trigger aggression.**

**Tone of voice: can also trigger aggression as you are not levelling the volume you speak at.**

**What you say: can trigger an automatic escalation as the attacker maybe using this to signal a response.**

**Alcohol and drugs: may trigger the attacker as they are not thinking rationally**

### INHIBITORS

**Personal beliefs: the attacker may be inhibited by their own personal beliefs from upbringing**

**Consequence: the attacker may be fearful of consequence from a legal or moral point of view**

**De-escalation: your de-escalation may be effective enough to negate an escalation**

**Confidence: a confident attitude may inhibit**

The main point in de-escalation is to be calm and speak in a non aggressive manner which is synonymous with the stance you adopt.

### 3. Distraction

If communication and de-escalation is not working then a certain amount of distraction may give you the edge to exit the situation or to prepare for your defence. We have already discussed pattern interruption which is a combination of psychological refocusing by verbal stimulus; this in itself is one form of distraction. The other methods of distraction are:

1. Verbal distracting
   Is not when you say such terms as "look a flying pig" and hope they look for one, but the way you relate an answer to the verbal questioning that takes their focus away from you.

Just like we explained in communication when the attacker said "What the fu** you looking at?", and you respond with distractions such as "It's Paul isn't it, from school?", you have distracted their chain of thought.

2. Physical passive with dialogue
   Physical passive is the way you gesture with your body to take the focus of the attacker away from you. When you point at something and ask people a question about it, their first action is to look at what you are pointing at and then answer verbally, this is a physical distraction that is passive.

3. Physical active

Physical active should only be used in two circumstances:

1. *Potential multiple attackers.*

2. *When you have the honest belief that your life is in immediate danger and all other means of conflict management have failed.*

The physical active is basically a pre-emptive strike to shock the attacker, which also can have aggressive dialogue associated with it. The physical shock tactics will be covered in more detail in defence, however it is the parts of the body that can be struck in such a fashion as to not seriously damage but have a pain response of critical focus for the attacker which distracts their initial attack on you. A simple palm slap full frontal to the face can be one method, as the attacker immediately steps back and his hands cover the painful area, the face and the eyes well, instantly affecting their vision. This physical distraction may give you time to escape or deal with another attacker.

4. Both physical and verbal combination.

This can be a combination of both but ensure that you are aware of combining the two so that you don't send out mixed intentions. For instance if you decide to use physical active and pre-empt a strike, don't use soft words and apologise afterwards, be aggressive and larger than life as the reason you are using physical active is that you feel that your life is in danger. The same for the opposite, don't use harsh and aggressive words if you are just going to slap their hand as the language and tone is not synonymous with the amount of force used.

## 4. Defend

Once past distraction you need to be in a position to defend yourself and the options available will be covered in greater detail in the next module. Just remember our primary directive is avoidance and not to get into this position in the first place, however the defence module will take you through a scientific approach to defence strategies and tactics that may save your life.

## P – Prepare

Now you have created the options for choice then you need to prepare mentally and physically to carry out those options. This may be that you need to start moving or getting ready for the possibility of an attack or moving into a position that you can exit. Even though your body has been through the Control and Options phase naturally and instinctively, you will find that you are already prepared to make an exit or defend yourself.

## E – Eliminate

Eliminate F.E.A.R. by seeing a positive outcome of any exit or defence before it happens. This, as mentioned previously, relies on the mental blueprinting of a scenario and the knowledge you have with dealing with such situations. As we said before knowledge dispels fear.

## Summary

So the C.O.P.E. tool of options guides you through the natural progression of a situation and stands for:

**Control** Yourself and your environment

**Options** Create options through the following:

| | |
|---|---|
| 1. Communication | What blocks communication and how to effectively communicate with an attacker |
| 2. De-escalation | How to de-escalate by removing triggers and finding inhibitors |
| 3. Distraction | By using verbal and physical distractions you may be able to create time for greater options |
| 4. Defence | This module will be covered later |

**Prepare** Yourself mentally and physically

**Eliminate** Eliminate F.E.A.R. by visualization

## THINK POINT DEFUSE 4

### 4.1 EXPLAIN THE FOUR STEPS OF THE OPTIONS PROCESS (COPE) OF CONFLICT MANAGEMENT

SEE YOUR INSTRUCTOR FOR WORKSHEET (IF YOU ARE TAKING EXAM)

# PROCEED

## "KNOWLEDGE DISPELS FEAR, AND CREATES CONFIDENCE TO EMPOWER YOU"

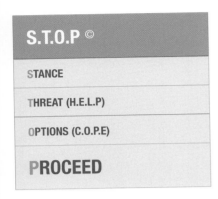

| S.T.O.P © |
| --- |
| STANCE |
| THREAT (H.E.L.P) |
| OPTIONS (C.O.P.E) |
| PROCEED |

By adopting the correct stance, assessing the threat and creating options you should be able to proceed with your actions by exiting the situation or defending yourself. Don't forget at any stage of the conflict management process your primary directive is avoidance, this should be what you aim for, not only from physical but also moral and legal consequence.

To reiterate on what the S.T.O.P conflict management emergency directive will enable you to achieve, firstly it is an autonomic system in that you will automatically and naturally go through these processes and secondly it is a directive (an order, instruction or guide) which minimises emotional thought and feeling and tries to bring you back into rational thought, which in turn brings your heart and breathing rate down and dampens your sympathetic nervous system which excretes adrenalin.

## THINK POINT DEFUSE 2

**2.1 EXPLAIN THE FOUR STEPS OF CONFLICT MANAGEMENT (S.T.O.P.) WITHIN THE R.A.I.D. (RAPID ACTION INITIATED DEFENCE) SYSTEM**

SEE YOUR INSTRUCTOR FOR WORKSHEET (IF YOU ARE TAKING EXAM)

# DEFEND

# R.A.I.D Defence Cycle / Rapid Action Initiated Defence

1 Confidence    2 Awareness    3 Conflict Management    4 Defence    5 Aftermath

**RATIONAL THOUGHT**

## DETER
Develop more confidence, through learning Specialist Skills, which will create a Non Victim mentality and provide you with a safer way of living.

## DETECT
Through Awareness and visual Observation skills, you will be able to foresee potential situations before they arise by subtle indicators or triggers.

## DEFUSE
By following our S.T.O.P conflict management process, you will be able to de-escalate the situation, whilst preparing the mind and body to Escape or Defend.

**EMOTIONAL THOUGHT**

## DEFEND
RAID Defence, works on the body's natural reflexes, which combined with universal defence concepts, make it easy to learn and remember when you need it most.

## DESENSITIZE
After a violent confrontation, you may suffer from denial or mental stress. We will provide the tools, techniques and advice to enable your recovery process.

PRE-ASSAULT (PRO-ACTIVE)    ASSAULT (RE-ACTIVE)    POST-ASSAULT (ACTIVE)

** This picture represents the processes of escalation from 1 to 5 of a physical confrontation unfolding

© 2008 to H2H Defence & CTR Services Ltd

# WELCOME TO DEFEND

**Founder/Chief Instructor**
Mr Tremaine Kent

Designed by Tremaine Kent, this is the final part of the escalation after you have detected and attempted to defuse the confrontation and you are not able to get away. In this module you will learn the physical elements of the tactical "C.O.P.E." process which allows you to reflexively cope with any physical assault you may encounter. The module is split into understandable segments starting with:

Knowledge Based - The knowledge based elements are by about understanding the body and what it can and can't do and what happens to you when it is attacked. You will also learn anatomy of defence, target areas of the anatomy and tools of the defence, so that you can protect yourself scientifically and economically. Through personal experience and self understanding.

Physical Based – the physical based element is split into four segments from Basic Combat Arts to know how to get those parts of the body working again and fight fitness. Minimum Force, Reasonable Force through to Force Continuum which deals with weapons defence.

ALL PHYSICAL ELEMENTS SHOULD BE COVERED PRACTICALLY AND THE MANUALS SERVE AS A THEORETICAL GUIDE.

# ANATOMY OF DEFENCE

## "TO KNOW YOUR BODY IS TO KNOW THE WEAKNESS IN YOUR ATTACKER'S ARMOUR"

### Introduction
Violence in most cases starts with an attack on the mind which initiates an emotional response. We have already discussed fear management and how the body reacts to stimulus. We will now look at the body from an internal scientific approach by understanding the nervous system, natural survival mechanism, target areas, tools of defence and rhythm, pace and leverage.

### Nervous System
The structure of the nervous system is made up of two parts which basically form the system devoted to information transmission. The branches of nervous system that we will discuss in detail are as follows:

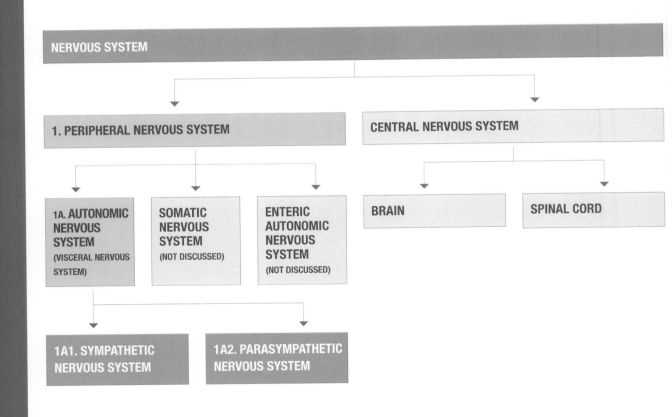

**NERVOUS SYSTEM**

**1. PERIPHERAL NERVOUS SYSTEM**

**CENTRAL NERVOUS SYSTEM**

**1A. AUTONOMIC NERVOUS SYSTEM** (VISCERAL NERVOUS SYSTEM)

**SOMATIC NERVOUS SYSTEM** (NOT DISCUSSED)

**ENTERIC AUTONOMIC NERVOUS SYSTEM** (NOT DISCUSSED)

**BRAIN**

**SPINAL CORD**

**1A1. SYMPATHETIC NERVOUS SYSTEM**

**1A2. PARASYMPATHETIC NERVOUS SYSTEM**

## 1. Peripheral Nervous System

The Peripheral Nervous System which branches outside of the Central Nervous System, is made up of three parts. The Autonomic Nervous System, Somatic Nervous System and the Enteric Nervous System. Sensory neurons running from receptors (parts of the body) send information to the brain and then motor neurons from the brain send information back to the muscles or glands (effectors) to take action. So when you place your hand over fire the sensors send information back to the brain which then sends information back to the hand and motor neurons to move it away.

## 1A. Autonomic Nervous System

The Autonomic Nervous System controls and regulates the body internally and its actions are largely involuntary. It is made up of cranial nerves that send impulses from the sensory organs to the brain, it regulates the increase and decrease rate of heartbeat as a response to stimulus, secretion of digestive fluids and the body's reaction to stress. The Autonomic Nervous System is split into two different parts: the Sympathetic Nervous System and the Parasympathetic Nervous System.

## 1A1. Sympathetic Nervous System

The Sympathetic Nervous System responds to impending danger or stress and is responsible for the increase of one's heart rate, blood pressure and is directly connected to the Adrenal Medulla, which in turn excretes what's commonly known as Adrenaline (Noradrenaline). The release of Noradrenaline:

- Stimulates heart rate
- Raises blood pressure
- Dilates pupils
- Shunts blood away from skin to the brain, heart and skeletal muscles
- Inhibits contraction of the bladder and rectum
- Inhibits saliva

In short the Sympathetic Nervous System prepares the body for emergencies; for fight or flight and triggers the survival mechanism with an increase in blood pressure and heart rate, larger muscles lose their fine motor skill functionality. The cognitive processing and visual performance are also hindered.

## 1A2. Parasympathetic Nervous System

The Parasympathetic Nervous System is responsible for the control of our actions and thoughts in a non stressful environment. It controls fine motor skills, cognitive processing and is also responsible for returning the body to normal after a Sympathetic stimulation. When the Parasympathetic Nervous System is stimulated through the Vagus Nerve it:

- Slows down the heartrate
- Lowers blood pressure
- Constriction of pupils
- Increase and releases blood flow to the skin and extremities
- Allows bowel movement to regain

In short when you practise traditional martial arts techniques you will be utilising the cognitive Parasympathetic Nervous System. This system is in direct conflict with the Sympathetic Nervous System which you will actually be using in an imminent violent confrontation. This creates a gap in what you instinctively and reflexively want to do (emotional – gross motor skills) and teachings taught in martial arts (cognitive rational – fine motor skills). Human instinct and the physical response will always predominate over your training.

THIS IS WHY YOU NEED TO WORK WITH YOUR INSTINCTIVE, REFLEXIVE RESPONSE TO SUDDEN VIOLENCE AND LEARN HOW TO DEFENSIVELY AND OFFENSIVELY BIND YOUR DEFENCE STRATEGY TO IT SO THAT THE NUCLEUS OF YOUR DEFENCE ARSENAL IS BASED ON YOUR CORE REFLEX, WHICH MAKES IT A NON PERISHABLE SKILL.

# STARTLE TO FLINCH MECHANISM

## Introduction

The flinch is a critically important protective mechanism by which humans instantly protect themselves against threats and violent attacks. It differs in many ways from situations from an emotional attack, because the body goes straight into survival mode which creates a reflexive flinch response to sudden stimulus. Within traditional arts and other systems, there seems to be a distinctive knowledge void in that some believe you can override or change the flinch mechanics through repetition of technique, to outright misunderstanding of how important the flinch mechanism is in self defence training.

Studies show and prove that the flinch mechanism is an automatic one that is not cognitively controlled (you don't need to think about it, it happens naturally) and that there are two distinct phases or parts to the whole process:

### 1. Phase 1

Initial Startled Reaction to Stimulus. The involuntary reflexive response to a sudden and unexpected stimulus which involves flexion of most skeletal muscles.

### 2. Phase 2

Longer Defensive Response. Directed toward the protection from a threat. To give you an analogy of this, imagine you are driving your car and a dog jumps out in front of you, your first response is the speed you reflexively hit the brake and the second is forcing the brake pedal through the floor.

## Flinch Blueprinting

The Rapid Action Initiated Defence Flinch Blueprinting is a unique conceptual method of combining your reflexive response to stimulus into your defence strategy, and developing a reduction in perception of incident time and gross motor skilled 360 degree defence concepts. To begin this exploration we need to look at certain criteria, for instance; does the reaction change when we are ready and waiting to be attacked, over not knowing the attack is going to happen, as this is crucial. The objectives you need to fulfil in training are:

### 1. Reaction or Flinch

You want to maximise the reaction time and make best use of the flinch which we said is part one and the hard wired non-controllable system. The way to do this is by trying to use the colour coding when you feel the environment is not safe so that you are already preparing for the potential of an attack, and also to adopt the correct posture for the environment (reactive stance).

### 2. Perception to Action

You want to minimise the time spent perceiving the incident before you react. This you can modify by working within training to live stimulus and flinch blueprinting.

Now to do this you need to find your natural flinch mechanism within your defence strategy. If you are mindful of the R.A.I.D. Cycle when in Deterrence and Defuse mode, you will be deemed as an aware individual to the potential of an attack and that the flinch and the reaction to flinch will obviously be a lot faster to a sudden attack or stimulus.

## Where does the flinch come from?

As previously mentioned the Central Nervous System is made up of the spinal cord and the brain. There is a part of the brain called the Limbic System, and in particular the Amygdala (the body's warning system) that is responsible for emotions, perception and voluntary movement. New studies have been conducted at Princeton University by Dylan Cooke and Michael Graziano from the psychology department into neural machinery that controls flinching by dialling the response up or down using drugs. Their studies concentrated on a region of the motor cortex which appears to react to stimulus of impeding sudden danger approaching the body, and they conclude that this area of the brain provides insight into how our bodies function when defending itself. In layman's terms the stimulus of an attack whether visual, audible or tactical is sent to the Limbic System and in particularly Amygdala (reptilian brain) and then zipped to the motor cortex to make the body go into action, flinch and react.

From a training and learning aspect when the flinch does occur, there is a reflexive creating distance and what I mean by this is that if you walked in a room and someone jumped out on you, you would instinctively step or jump backwards and away from the threat. When this occurs in a violent situation, by stepping, jumping back or reflexively creating distance you are allowing the aggressor the opportunity to have another go. So the reduction in perception of incident time you develop in training should allow you to acknowledge the first flinch and close the distance rapidly, which in turn will increase your survivability.

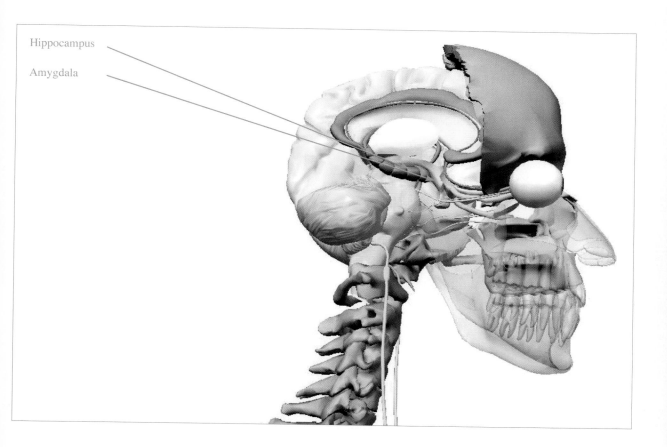

Hippocampus

Amygdala

## THINK POINT DEFEND 1

1.1 EXPLAIN HOW THE BODY REACTS TO CONFRONTATION
1.2 EXPLAIN WHY THE STARTLE TO FLINCH MECHANISM IS IMPORTANT IN SELF DEFENCE

SEE YOUR INSTRUCTOR FOR WORKSHEET (IF YOU ARE TAKING EXAM)

# TARGET AREAS OF THE BODY

### Introduction

Surviving the street is a matter of being smart and yet to a degree, ruthless. This may require you to use deception in your approach by looking passive, to go for the right body targets for that particular situation. After all there is no point spending time on a powerful punch technique if you hit the attacker in the behind, whereas a strike to the throat needs less power and has a lasting effect on the aggressor. We appreciate there are many areas of the body which are vulnerable and have an effect to pain or manipulation. This session will identify the three major target areas: Primary (Attitude Adjustments), Secondary (Less-Lethal Targets) and Tertiary (Lethal Targets), in relation to use of force and the destructive capability.

### Primary Targets – green areas

Primary targets may be utilized if you need to stimulate movement to use secondary or tertiary targets or if you require the bare minimum amount of force in order to escape or adjust a person's attitude towards a confrontational situation. As mentioned previously there are obviously many other target areas and it is not our intention to list all of them, we merely want to point out areas that will be used in later modules.

### Secondary Targets – amber areas

Secondary targets are commonly used when a less lethal means of defensive strategy can be employed. If under the use of force you are in danger of attack but it is not life threatening then these target areas may be used to defend yourself in order to get away or disengage. You should not continue force when it is clear that you have the opportunity to escape.

### Tertiary Targets – red areas

Tertiary targets may be utilized if you are facing an imminent lethal attack and you have every legal right to defend yourself using this amount of force and to the areas described. Only you can decide if this is appropriate defence force to use, so be fully aware of consequence.

HIGH FORCE

HIGH FORCE

TERTIARY TARGET

SECONDARY TARGET

PRIMARY TARGET

LOW FORCE

LOW FORCE

**Nose** Nasal injuries cause heavy bleeding, uncontrollable eye-watering and intense pain. A palm strike to the nose or manipulation by inserting fingers into the nose makes opponents pull away, and is generally a more-effective self-defence technique than trying to gouge his eyes.

**Spinal Cord** Any damage to the spinal cord or any cervical vertebrae causes paralysis or death. Instantaneous death is most likely after breaks above the third cervical vertebrae or between the fifth and sixth thoracic vertebrae. (These spots are at the top of the neck, about where the spine enters the skull, and directly between the shoulder blades.)

**The Carotid Sinus and Vagus Nerves** The carotid arteries carry blood to your brain. The vagus nerves regulate your heartbeat and breathing. They coincide at a point on the neck just below the angle of the jaw. Light blows to carotid sinus cause the victim to faint within seconds, while heavy blows cause certain severe damage. All blows to the carotid sinus are dangerous due to a greatly increased risk of stroke following undiagnosed arterial wall disintegration.

**Bone on Bone** Areas of shoulders, sternum and back of hands – quick direct strikes with your knuckles will cause a pain reflex, normally resulting in avoidance of the area of pain.

**Knees** As the knees act as a fundamental part of movement, the misconceptions of damaging the knee by a kick needs to be looked at in more detail. For the patella (kneecap), to be broken, the knee has to be both locked and weight-bearing. This will be unusual outside of sporting activities. The best way and most economic way to damage the knee is by kicking the leg from the inside out, this will damage the cruciate ligaments. The cruciate ligaments cross the knee in an X and are located behind the kneecap. The pain reflex if damaged will immobilise the leg.

**Head Frontal Left and Right Lobes** These are at the front of the head, when slapped will cause a shudder through the head normally causing an instantaneous headache and disorientation.

**Instep and toes** The small bones and tendons in the foot are easily hurt, particularly by powerful downward blows. High-heeled shoes are particularly notorious in this regard. The pain reflex for a non-aware attacker is to bend and cover the painful area. Be aware that this may not be effective if the attacker is under the influence of drugs or emotionally disturbed.

**Ears** Slapping the ears with cupped hands ruptures the victim's eardrums. This causes the victim to suffer hearing loss, light-headedness, and balance problems until his eardrums heal. The external part of the ear also can be bitten or twisted, and bleeds profusely. Treatment generally requires rest and surgery.

**Eyes and Ears** Spitting into the eyes will cause an automatic flinch reflex. Shouting into the ears will also cause the head to move away.

**Eyes** While finger strikes to the eyes cause great pain and terror, serious eye injuries rarely result from them. The reason is that everyone instinctively jerks away from attacks to their eyes.

**Front of Neck** Chokes and strikes to the front of the neck can shut off the carotid arteries. This can cause unconsciousness. Meanwhile, attacks that damage the windpipe cause death through suffocation.

**Point of the Chin** Knuckles break on chins. However, the heel of your palm doesn't. Upward blows with the heel of the palm to the point of the chin sever tongues and break teeth, while exceptionally powerful blows cause brain concussion and whiplash.

**Fingers** When using breakaway concepts the fingers are the weakest part of the attackers arsenal and will be the easiest point to break free.

**Genitals** Both men and women can have damage caused to their genital areas. Because they are filled with countless tiny blood vessels, penises and labia are better bitten or cut than crushed. However, flicking hits and sharp yanks to the testicles cause nauseating pain.

**Ankles** The Achilles tendon is permanently damaged by stomping kicks and lacerations from behind. This area is an effective secondary target if you are on the ground and the attacker is stood up. It is also the base of a lever to bring the attacker to ground.

---

# THINK POINT DEFEND 2

**2.1 PERFORM A PHYSICAL DEMONSTRATION OF THE TARGET AREAS OF THE BODY AND SUMMARISE THE WAYS IN WHICH THESE AREAS REACT TO PAIN.**

SEE YOUR INSTRUCTOR FOR WORKSHEET (IF YOU ARE TAKING EXAM)

# TOOLS OF DEFENCE

## "DO NOTHING WHICH IS OF NO USE"
### MUSASHI

### Introduction

There are many of you who know how to use your anatomy to hit, kick or punch and even fitness training such as boxercise and other martial arts orientated sessions try to develop a certain amount of these skills. However in this element we want to clarify what is and isn't effective on the street and the pros and cons for each. We have broken the tools into ranges, which are kicking range, punching range, close quarters range and ground range. This is not an exhaustive list but merely the basics and will be covered practically during sessions.

### Kicking Range

Kicks can be powerful if used in a correct manner, however as this is a long range tool and it forms the base of your balance, in a real situation do you want to be bringing one leg off the floor and interfering with balance and stability? Also as this requires the largest muscle group you may certainly telegraph your intentions. You will see a lot of attackers kicking victims when they are on the ground and the types are stomps and football toe punts, rather than professional martial arts kicks not to mention the environment may not lend itself to any fancy kicking.

| PROS | CONS |
|------|------|
| • LONG WEAPON | • POOR BALANCE |
| • LOW LINE ATTACKS | • SHOWS BODY INTENTIONS |
| • POWERFUL | • HIGH ENERGY NEEDED |

### Punching Range

On the streets of today the most common attack is the sucker punch or the hay maker as they rely on gross motor skills and attackers presume that the faster and harder they throw the punch the better and more effective it will be. However this couldn't be further from the truth. The biggest point we should identify is it is more effective to PALM strike than punch, you can generate just as much force with a palm as you can with a punch and the legal consequence could be significantly lower.

| PROS | CONS |
|------|------|
| • SPEED AND MORE ANGLES (PALMS) | • EGO BASED |
| • QUARTER BEAT CONTINUUM | • HEAD HUNTING |
| • STABLE PLATFORM AND BALANCE | • DAMAGED KNUCKLES IF PUNCHING |

## Close Quarters Range

Without doubt the most important range and one that is surrounded by controversy, in that most attackers will be in or travel through to attack you and thus this should be the base and foundation of your learning. Also by reading the previous manuals you will have noticed that most street violence or any realistic attack starts physically from this range.

Due to the close proximity of this range your tactile sensitivity, psychological and conflict management skills need to be fine-tuned as the hand is quicker than the eye and your perception of incident for any attack action by an aggressor needs to be fast and in tune with your instinctive natural reflexes.

### PROS

- ALL THE MAIN TARGETS ARE CLOSE
- LEAST BODY INTENTION
- CONFLICTS START IN THIS RANGE
- TACTILE SENSITIVITY
- YOU HAVE MORE OPTIONS
- STABLE PLATFORM AND BALANCE

### CONS

- HAND IS QUICKER THAN THE EYE
- PERCEPTION OF INCIDENT NEEDS TO BE FAST
- YOU ARE VULNERABLE AT LOW LEVEL
- CONCEALED WEAPONS

## Ground Range

A lot of martial artists say 80% of fights go to ground but surely 100% start from the standing position. This range also falls into the grappling range as this normally is the way you make it to the ground. The energy created in this range is powerful and can be very dangerous.

Now there are two concepts I want you to consider and the first is if you have taken the attacker to the ground why aren't you escaping? And second, if you find yourself on the floor then you need to get up as fast as possible. If the latter happens then you have to be able to defend whilst you try to get up and preferably within a few seconds.

### PROS

- YOUR ESCAPE CAN BE FAST IF ATTACKER IS DOWN
- TACTILE SENSITIVITY
- LACK OF KNOWLEDGE IN RANGE FOR ATTACKER

### CONS

- IF YOU ARE ON THE GROUND BE CONSCIOUS OF THIRD PARTIES
- THE ATTACKER HAS TACTILE SENSITIVITY
- CONCEALED WEAPONS

# RHYTHM, PACE & LEVERAGE

## Rhythm and Pace

If you consider most attacks on the street, or especially in the ring you will normally see a rhythm and pace that the attack is being delivered by. Even in training the coaches or trainers get their students to strike focus mitts or shields to the count of 1 – 2, and in combinations so you can see the gap between each strike. The types of rhythm and pace have been designated terms which depending on what system you follow depends on the name.

The common terms used by the R.A.I.D system are natural, half-beat, quarter-beat and simultaneous. So that you understand the differences between each of them the diagrams below show the natural and quarter-beat (which is the preferred rhythm of defensive attack you should employ).

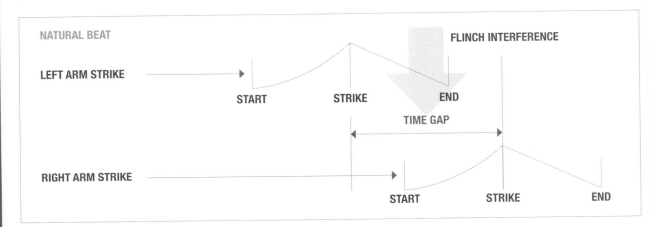

The natural beat diagram above shows the time gap between each strike, which in real terms means that once the first strike has connected, by the time the second starts the natural reflexes or the flinch mechanism of the attacker steps in and they can now counter the next strike, keeping them in control and with a predator mentality.

Let's now look at the preferred rhythm of defensive mythology taught to R.A.I.D students and the reasons why we teach this rhythm and pace:

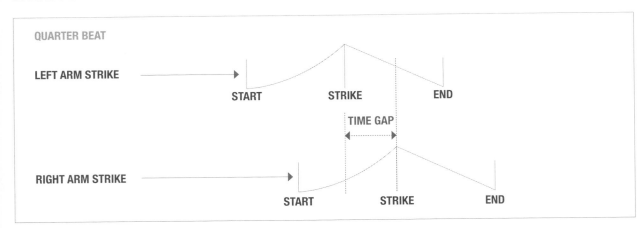

As you can see from the diagram above (quarter beat) the time gap between each strike is a lot less, which means that the flinch interference by the attacker is a lot harder to achieve, which places more pressure on them and their original predator mentality is now back pedalling and they are now working on defence and prey mentality.

## "CLOSE IS STRONG, LONG IS WEAK"

### Leverage

Another important principle to understand is leverage and how your body can use it to aid in your defence mythology. Whether you are working in Close Quarters Range or defending with minimal force from a wrist grab, the principle of leverage will always apply. You have to consider that you don't know the size or strength of an attacker and use your body's leverage for the worst possible scenario.

If we look at the saying "close is strong and long is weak" in more detail from the pictures below:

### Close is Strong

The attacker in black tries to force down on the defenders arm from a long lever, against the bent arm of the defender which is close to the chest. Because the attacker is working away from his body he is reliant on skeletal muscles that are extended to the maximum. So the energy used by the defender is remarkably less than the attacker.

Now if you consider that the attacker has his arm around your neck and you have hold of the arm, the principle is the same and you have the advantage (he is long and you are short)

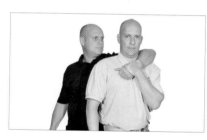

**LONG ARM AROUND THE BODY**

**SHORT BENT ARMS CLOSE TO THE BODY**

### Long is Weak

The attacker in black is now short and the defender is long, which has the opposite effect and one which you do not want to be in a position of if you can avoid it. So to put it into real terms, if the attacker had a knife in his hand, he would not only have the edge over power, but also leverage and the defender would not be able to control the situation as he is long and weak.

This can be avoided in many cases which will be covered in later elements and practical sessions.

# MINIMUM FORCE

### Introduction to Grabs

From previous modules, you have discovered that the law and legal consequence has a major part in your defence method and that you cannot attack from an attack with greater force. This first element is based on the minimum amount of force synonymous to minor physical altercations of grabs. Let's say you are trying to de-escalate a situation and another person or third party grabs your clothing, this doesn't now give you the legal right to punch them with all the power you have, as this is not reasonable nor justifiable in the eyes of the law.

### The Problem

The picture on the right outlines the problem of a basic lapel grab, but could be a body grab and could be from the side or the back. Now if we break down this problem in more detail, the potential dangers that this could lead onto can escalate out of control of minimum force very quickly. Here are a few problems we have:

- You are now connected to the attacker.
- The attacker has a certain amount of control over you.
- The hand holding you can strike at short distance.
- You can not deal with third party attackers.
- If grabbed from the back you cannot identify the threat.

### TYPES OF GRAB

**WRIST BODY GRAB**

**COLLAR CLOTHING GRAB**

**COLLAR CLOTHING GRAB**

### The Solution – Guiding Principles

You should have a minimum force contingency to deal with such problems that are common on the streets in many different environments and scenarios that allow you to break free and prepare your position for immediate escalation. Within other systems and traditional arts they tend to address these problems by having many different techniques for each angle you are attacked from. This type of defence is not inline with instinctive training and that is why you need to adopt a conceptual defence system. The guiding principles you need to adopt will enable you to take some control back safely and break away successfully without escalating the situation.

#### 1. Communicate

Start to communicate immediately and that means listening to what's being said.

#### 2. Tactile Guard Sensitivity

Adopt a reactive stance and try to reach some form of tactile sensitivity.

### 3. Weak Point & Create Space

On most grabs the weak point is the fingers holding you and to create space is manipulating yourself into a position where they are long and you are short.

### 4. Rotate or Leverage

With the created space and the weak link you can rotate your body or a limb to provide you with body weight leverage over the grip.

### Introduction to Holds

Unlike grabs when the hands are used, holds concentrate on being held by the attacker's arms. The common term for this is classed as bear hugs. Again there is no real threat to life at this stage and depending on the hold depends on the amount of force and leverage used, but remember you do not want to escalate the situation further. To give you an analogy of this, in a scenario an attacker comes from behind you and holds you round the waist encapsulating the arms. Without any other information the defence is straight forward.

### The Problem

The picture on the right outlines the problem of a basic bear hug with arms captured or inside, but this could be from front, side, arms on the outside or any combination. Now if we break down this problem in more detail, the potential dangers that this could lead onto can escalate out of control of minimum force very quickly, as this form of hold on the street is associated with multiple attackers. Here are a few problems we have:

- You are now connected to the attacker.

- The attacker has a certain amount of control over you.

- Your balance and stability is in the attackers hands.

- You cannot deal with third party attackers.

### TYPES OF HOLD

**OPEN – FRONT BEAR HUG**

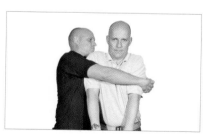

**CLOSED – SIDE BEAR HUG**

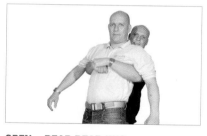

**OPEN – REAR BEAR HUG**

### The Solution – Guiding Principles

Even though you will have a minimum force contingency to deal with such problems you have to be aware of the scenario and environment in which the hold is used. Again you need to get away from techniques, as the variation of the holds create too many defences. That is why you need to be conceptual in your approach.

The guiding principles you should adopt will enable you to take some control back safely and breakaway successfully without escalating the situation out of proportion (unless you have to).

### 1. Communicate
Start to communicate immediately and that means listening to what's being said.

### 2. Create Space
Using leverage or an attitude adjustment.

### 3. Weak Point & Guard
Break the weak point and adopt an instant guard or reactive stance.

### 4. Rotate or Leverage
With the break in the hold, you may be able to rotate out or use leverage (in some cases use the head to push away from).

### Introduction to Attitude Adjustments
With regards to grabs and holds, we mentioned about attitude adjustments in order to create space, well creating space is the prime directive of attitude adjustments. The creation of space is merely by working on the attacker's startle to flinch mechanism and pain survival reflex that everyone has. By applying direct minimum force or overloading the sensors the attacker's flinch will automatically kick in and their body will react.

### COMMON ATTITUDE ADJUSTMENTS

#### The Face Slap
With an open palm, slap the face and nose with a short sharp shock. This will automatically make the eyes water and cause the person to step back.

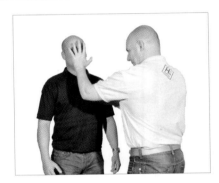

#### The Hand Jab
With a clenched fist, rap or place direct pressure onto the attacker's grip, if it is fast and sharp the pain will ease the grip or hold for a second. This can be used on closed bear hugs, hair grabs and many other grabs or holds.

### Minimum Force Conclusion
To conclude this element and the first part of physical defence, minimum force is exactly what it implies and it is the next progression above conflict management, but seen as a de-escalating way of dissolving the situation and breaking away, hence the term "Breakaway Concepts".

## THINK POINT DEFEND 3

**3.1 PERFORM A PHYSICAL DEMONSTRATION OF THE DEFENCE AGAINST A GRAB OR A HOLD.**

SEE YOUR INSTRUCTOR FOR WORKSHEET (IF YOU ARE TAKING EXAM)

# REASONABLE FORCE

### Introduction

This element concentrates on physical attacks through the previously mentioned ranges (kicking, punching, close quarters and ground ranges). So why have we classified these ranges as reasonable force? Well the answer is in the law and just to refresh you, the law states, "a person may use force as is reasonable in the circumstances in prevention of crimes". With the types of attacks through these ranges you may be dealing with common assault to GBH or worse.

We will look at each range from longest to shortest identifying the problem and looking at concept solutions that work 360 degree, multifunctional and with the primary directive of escape in mind and not escalation as seen in many other systems. If the truth be known as soon as an attacker no longer has the Means, Opportunity or Intent then your defence must drop down to be justifiable. I once saw an instructor teaching a defence against a lapel grab, who completed a fantastic technique that impressed his students then after the fourth or fifth punch to the face he then took the attacker to the ground and stamped on his throat. Is this justifiable? No wonder so many who defend themselves end up getting sued or even put behind bars.

### THE RANGES AND DEFENCES

| KICKING | PUNCHING | CLOSE QUARTERS | GROUND |
|---|---|---|---|
|  |  |  |  |
| **FRONT DEFENCE**<br>**SIDE DEFENCE** | **JAB DEFENCE**<br>**SUCKER PUNCH DEFENCE** | **HEADBUTT DEFENCE**<br>**ELBOW STRIKES DEFENCE**<br>**KNEE STRIKES DEFENCE**<br>**TAKE DOWNS DEFENCE**<br>**COMMON ATTACKS DEFENCE** | **MOUNTED DEFENCE**<br>**NON-MOUNTED DEFENCE**<br>**THIRD PARTY DEFENCE** |

# KICKING RANGE DEFENCE
# LONG RANGE

### The Problem
The problems you face from kicks are that they utilise the body's largest muscle group, which can create an enormous amount of force. You also are kept at some distance so any reasonable counter defence from the punching or medium range will be ineffective. This being said, on the street you are more likely to be kicked on the floor and below the waist than by any fancy martial arts kicks.

### The Solution – Guiding Principles
We have established the problems associated with kicks, now working within reasonable force we need to have a method of defence against them. The two types of defence concepts you can employ are as follows:

### 1. Deflection
Your natural reflexes want you to move away so don't deny this but add to it by using an arm to deflect at the same time.

### 2. Identify Triggers
A lot of attackers generally work on bigger harder force and as such tend to telegraph their intentions. By knowing how and what the triggers are will allow you to move away and out of reach of the potential kick.

# PUNCHING RANGE DEFENCE
# MEDIUM RANGE

### The Problem
Most probably the most common form of attack on the street and again the punches you have seen on the street are not the same as you see in a boxing ring. With regards to punching the major cause of injury is the sucker punch (hay maker or open hook punch) which comes from the side. This form of punch means the person is actually within the close quarters range due to power created with the arm bent and the shoulder movement, and the fact that attackers feel they can hit harder in this way. Also be aware of combinations or repetitions of strikes.

### The Solution – Guiding Principles
Whilst being in a passive but reactive stance let your body's natural reflexes take over and under the guidance of reasonable force and the law, once you have negated the strike be conscious of any counters you may wish to do. The guiding principles you should adopt will enable you to negate a majority of punches naturally from the reactive stance:

### 1. Reactive Stance
Your natural reflexes and startle to flinch from the reactive stance will automatically defend against most strikes. By placing the hands within your centre line (centre of the body) you are creating a psychological void in the eyes of the attacker which forces them to sucker punch.

### 2. Trap and Control
Once a sucker punch has been thrown and your natural defence reflexively blocks the punch, trap the arm or shoulder and immobilise the body by disrupting the cognitive brain response (covered in close quarters range) or taking the attacker to the ground.

# GROUND RANGE DEFENCE
## GROUND RANGE

### The Problem

The two main problems we have from the ground are: 1. being taken down to the ground and 2. defending with the attacker on top of you (mount position) and defending whilst on the ground from attackers still standing.

### Take down

On a take down you need to consider the environment and what you are being taken down onto. There have been many accounts of people who have died just because they have knocked their heads on a curb, object or hard surface.

### On the ground

If you are on the ground and you face attackers that are still standing, the dangers to you are extreme, especially from stomps and kicks not from one attacker but third party attackers. This is so common on the streets as the cowards that come from nowhere and stamp on you and then disappear into the crowd.

### The Solution – Guiding Principles

In both cases and variants, the need to get off the ground should be your primary directive (within a few seconds). You also need to protect the vital areas of the body such as the head and spine. The four defence concepts you can employ are as follows:

#### 1. Sprawl

If an attacker tries to take you down, you need to jam and spread your weight which will minimise or potentialy negate you going to ground.

#### 2. Guard

When you are on the ground your natural reflexes want you to move into a form of the foetal position which is good to some degree; however it can leave your back and spine exposed, so be flexible and change your position with the environment.

#### 3. Close Distance

If the attacker is on you try to close the distance between you to minimise the torque they can create and also the closer to the attacker's head you are the less of a target you become from third party.

#### 4. Get Up

As we mentioned before the primary directive is to get up from the ground. In order to do this you need to guard yourself whilst doing this.

# CLOSE QUARTERS DEFENCE
# CLOSE QUARTERS RANGE

## The Problem

As previously mentioned this is the most common range of attack. The attacker needs to be close enough to attack you and in most cases once the delivery system (verbal or physical) has been initiated, the attacker will be more egotistically minded or intimidating depending on the form of attack and the victim's gender, which can leave their defences down. There are many forms of attack that you can fall foul of, however we have identified a few common ones.

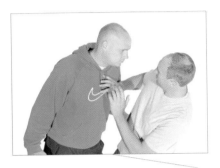

**HEADBUTT**

**ELBOW STRIKE**

**KNEE STRIKE**

**REACTIVE STANCE**

## THE PRINCIPLES OF R.A.I.D CLOSE QUARTER DEFENCE

**1 DIRECT**

"THE SHORTEST DISTANCE BETWEEN TWO POINTS IS A STRAIGHT LINE" BRUCE LEE.

THIS MAKES YOUR DEFENCE ECONOMIC AND STRAIGHT TO THE SENSES AREA OF THE BODY.

**2 SENSES**

ALL THE SENSES CONNECT DIRECT TO THE BRAIN (VULNERABLE POINT) AND BY OVERLOADING THEM AT SOURCE, CHANGES THE ATTACKER'S PREDATOR – PREY MENTALITY, WHICH DESTROYS COGNITIVE BRAIN FUNCTION.

## The Solution – Guiding Principles

In a lot of cases just being in the reactive stance will deny not only access but also the opportunity for a certain attack, due to the psychological void (physical barrier) it provides. As well as this we also have the guiding principles of R.A.I.D's Close Quarter Defence system which has four concepts: Direct, Senses, Tactile and Escape, highlighted below and discussed in more detail later.

**CHOKES***

**HEADLOCKS***

**TAKEDOWNS**

**REACTIVE STANCE**

THE PRINCIPLES OF R.A.I.D CLOSE QUARTER DEFENCE

**ONCE YOU HAVE INITIATED YOUR DEFENCE YOU NEED TO KEEP THE ATTACKER CLOSE AND KEEP TACTILE SENSITIVITY IN ORDER TO HAVE A 360 DEGREE AWARENESS.**

**3 TACTILE**

**ALLOWS YOU TO BE MINDFUL OF THE ENVIRONMENT SO THAT YOU MAY DISENGAGE AND ESCAPE FROM THE SITUATION AS SAFELY AS POSSIBLE.**

**4 ESCAPE**

* Chokes and Headlocks will also be covered in more detail due to the dangers they create

# R.A.I.D'S CLOSE QUARTER DEFENCE SYSTEM

## Introduction

Now you understand the importance of the reactive stance within close quarters range, you need to further understand the principles of the behavioural defence system. It is true that technical, rational teachings are less likely to function in high stress states and within the close quarters range your perception of incident doesn't allow you the time to rationally remember these teachings. So your defence methodology must work in unison with the startle to flinch gross motor skill system. To do this you will always find yourself doing something you have no knowledge of and when questioned, "Why did you do that?" The answer will most probably be, "I don't know, it just happened". The way you combine the body's natural survival mechanism with your defence strategy, is to follow guiding principles and concepts. The R.A.I.D. system has four principles to follow which are Direct, Senses, Tactile and Escape, explained in more detail below:

## Direct

"The shortest distance between two points is a straight line," as once said by the famous Bruce Lee. Well this is an interesting statement, in that if you read into it in more detail you will discover many other connected principles that are equally important such as economy of motion, non body intent movements and the closest weapon for the closest vulnerable point. So to go into it in more detail, if you look at a situation where you are in the reactive stance the following applies and works with your natural reactions.

### Attacker

They swing to punch you and as you are in the reactive stance, the punches are thrown to the outside of your hands to the side of the head.

### You

Your natural flinch mechanism sends your closest arm up to stop the impending danger, there is no fancy technical application, just pure instinct. Once this startle to flinch has happened, your perception of incident is faster than normal as you are working with your body's natural instincts and not against them, you then use the other tools to your arsenal and quarter beat initiate a defence move that is direct and straight to the vulnerable point without showing your body's intentions.

### Attacker

Due to your perception of incident from the flinch and the quarter beat defence response, which has not been shown through your body you are now one step closer to placing the attacker into defence mode (changing the attackers mentality from predator to prey).

### Conclusion

So when Bruce Lee developed Jet Kun Do (JKD), this principle of being direct is a fundamental principle on the street, as most attackers believe that the more torque and distance they use the more power they will create. However this is not the most direct and economical way, and also it doesn't matter how hard they believe their attack to be if it doesn't connect with the target.

## Senses

With the knowledge gained in previous elements regarding vulnerable points and when you may use such targets in the eyes of the law and which are synonymous to the level of danger you are placed in by the attacker, you will have identified that all the five senses connect directly to the brain and that they all have the survival mindset of protecting at all costs. By attacking these areas above the shoulder line you will override the attacker's rational and emotional brain functions and change their predator mentality to being the prey.

To state the obvious, if the attacker can't see you, how can they attack you. The concept you should follow is like that of the Kali (Indonesian) system, in that you need to bombard the senses so that they overload and the survival instinct of the attacker is one of defence and disengagement from the situation. Short quarter beat attacks to the vulnerable parts of the head will disorientate and debilitate the cognitive brain of your attacker and render them powerless over their own survival mechanisms. The severity of your attack can be passive without injury or in the case of fighting for your life then you may actively attack the areas that cause automatic debilitation.

## Tactile

As soon as you make contact with the attacker, you automatically gain tactile sensitivity which allows you to feel the energy in the attacker through touch and feeling. Why is this important I hear you say? Well if the attacker's energy is strong and working against yours, you will feel this and go with them as well as being able to predict their next movement. Don't work against their force as you can create a flinch by attacking a vulnerable point so that they move or open themselves to your way of thinking. You will also be able to feel through tactile sensitivity any movement of the attacker if they

attempt to pull a weapon out on you or try some form of attack due to you being passive in your initial nature. To understand this in simple terms, if you imagine that the head which holds all the senses is a ball of metal then your hands are magnets, and no matter what your position is in relation to the attacker your magnet hands will always search out the metal head and stick to it (tactically tactile). There are many training drills to develop tactile sensitivity and eventually you will be able to deal with an attacker physically whilst concentrating on your environment and escape routes.

## Escape

The last principle of escape has always been your primary directive, but by this stage you have not been able to. Once you have changed the predator-prey mentality of the attacker you should now be thinking of disengagement and escape. There are too many so called self

defence systems that carry on attacking the attacker until they are on the ground and even then they finish with a stamp on the throat, which is not reasonable and deemed excessive in the eyes of the law. You should immediately disengage and head for an escape route. This is also the time to use any personal protection alarm systems you may have and get to the nearest help.

## Conclusion

To conclude this close quarter defence system, if you follow the guiding principles you will be able to destroy the attacker's cognitive brain response, disorientate and unbalance them whilst overloading their senses with quarter beat attacks that can be both Active (damaging and debilitating) or Passive (with no physical damage or injury). There is no technical application needed and thus all of the movements you do are gross motor skills and non-choreographed.

---

## THINK POINT DEFEND 4

**4.1 PERFORM A PHYSICAL DEMONSTRATION OF THE DEFENCE AGAINST::**
   **A) A LONG RANGE ATTACK**
   **B) A MEDIUM RANGE ATTACK**
   **C) A CLOSE QUARTER'S RANGE ATTACK**
   **D) A GROUND RANGE ATTACK**
**4.2 PERFORM A PHYSICAL SCENARIO OF AN ATTACK TO DEVELOP MENTAL BLUEPRINTING.**

SEE YOUR INSTRUCTOR FOR WORKSHEET (IF YOU ARE TAKING EXAM)

# CHOKES

### Introduction
Unlike many other close quarters attacks the chokes are very important within defence as they can represent a danger to life. We know that if you cut off the air or blood supply to the brain you will die. Now

I agree in some circumstances that chokes are more frequent in certain attacks than others but due to the importance of the danger you have to have a realistic defence system that works with the natural instincts and takes no technical application to achieve.

### The Problem
The pictures below outline the problems of basic two handed chokes. These forms of attack can be anything from a confined space attack to a women being

sexually assaulted, the big problem this creates is the lack of time to defend, in that it only takes a matter of split seconds or millimetres to damage the windpipe and stop the air supply.

The other point to note is that there are so many variants of this attack, from one handed, from the rear, from the ground or from the side to mention a few.

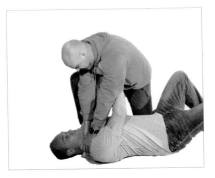

### The Solution – Guiding Principles
As this form of attack can be 360 degrees and critically dangerous, we have to rely on the natural instincts and not on technical teachings. When the attack is initiated your natural instinct is to arch your body away from the attack and your hands come up to the throat. Your aim is to break the

grip on your throat as safely and as quickly as possible. The throat is the connection between the head and the rest of the body and has the shape of a cylinder, now if you have ever tried holding and gripping a pole that is turning with leverage, the only way you can keep hold of it and stop it from turning is if your grip is stronger than the rotational

force. A lot of systems try to break the grip with external force which doesn't work in real situations as your brain will not compute a technical application. The guiding principles of A,B,C you need to adopt will enable you to effectively break the grip with the minimum amount of effort and control the attacker.

**A  Airway**
First thing you should do is raise the shoulders, this will allow a certain amount of space to be created for later movement and give you a small amount of airway control.

**B  Break**
To break the grip you need to rotate the shoulders and body in a fast rapid movement away from the attacker.

**C  Control or Clear**
Whilst breaking the grip raise an arm in the air so that your arm (bicep) touches the side of the head. This will allow you to catch and keep the attacker's arms when you rotate so that they cannot attack you again.

# HEADLOCKS

### Introduction

Just like the chokes, headlocks are very important within defence as they also represent a danger to life. The headlocks can cut the blood or air supply to the brain and as such present a problem of death. Now a lot of headlocks stem from grappling or when the attacker is trying to manipulate you and you resist against them. Again if the attacker gets a good hold around your neck you only have seconds to achieve a realistic defence.

### The Problem

The pictures below outline the problems of basic headlocks.

There are three forms that we will consider, they are rear, side and front headlocks.

The problem with most headlocks is that they are initiated from the rear and as such you may not have awareness until it is too late. As soon as they have their arm around your neck and under your chin you will feel pain and then panic, dependant on the type you will feel the head rush of lack of blood or the chocking reflex on your windpipe. By this time it is very difficult to do anything apart from panic. The other point to note is that there are so many variants of this attack, from being on the floor to being sat down to mention a few.

### The Solution – Guiding Principles

When the attack is initiated your natural instinct is to raise your hands to the throat and try to pull the threat away. Your primary aim is to deny the attacker from getting their arm under the chin and then to break the grip on your throat as safely and as quickly as possible. A lot of other systems try to attack another part of the attacker's anatomy or fight your way out, however from experience you will not have time to do any of these fancy moves as your survival mechanism is in full control. Just like chokes you need to adopt the A,B,C guiding principles as follows.

**A Airway**
To create a patent airway place your chin on your shoulder, this will deny both the blood and air chokes.

**B Break**
To give you more time you need to bring an arm up to brace the attacker's hold. This will deny the attacker to place more force on their attack.

**C Control or Clear**
There are numerous ways to break this hold but now you have given yourself time, the best form is by inflicting pain.

**CHAPTER 5 DEFEND**

# FORCE CONTINUUM

### Introduction

This element concentrates on multiple attackers and weapons defence. As these attacks may lead to serious wounding and even death, the level of defence used will normally require you to use tertiary attacks in order to defend yourself. Always be mindful of the law within the situation you find yourself in, however if you are in a life threatening situation and you have the true honest belief that you are in mortal danger your primary directive is one of survival.

Some of the attacks that you may fall into within force continuum range are group gang attacks where you are confronted by a group of individuals that are acting in a threatening manner, muggings where an edged weapon is used to take valuables by force, sexual attacks such as rape and firearms threats and attacks (theory only). The outcome of some of these attacks can result in serious wounding or even loss of life. The elements we will cover in more detail are as follows:

### Multiple Attacker Defence

In the UK gangs and group culture is ever increasing especially within inner city areas, the way music influences this glorified lifestyle has permeated itself on the impressions of the forgotten youth of today. This form of mentality can create a potentially disastrous situation for any victim that falls foul of an attack in that the level of violence seems to feed itself within a group, until the group are stopped abruptly or the victim has sustained a certain amount of injury, normally serious.

### Edged Weapons Awareness

This element starts by examining the definition of offensive weapons and the law surrounding them. You will then identify the types of edged weapons commonly used from man made, adapted or intended to be used as a weapon. From previous modules, if you have awareness of something you are more inclined to notice it and have a pre-emptive approach to dealing with a situation. Again the assumption rule is that the potential attacker is always armed.

### Edged Weapons Defence

There are two forms of defence that you should be aware of for edged weapons and they are: threats when someone wants something from you or they want you to comply, normally in the form of muggings, and attacks, when the intent is to cut, lacerate, slash or kill for purpose. Both of which can be fatal but defendable, by following some easy guiding principles. Remember no matter what you do you must always be prepared and expect to get cut.

### Firearms Awareness

We say firearms but we classify them as projectile weapons. This element is purely of understanding and will not cover the defences. You will look at the two types of handgun and the rifle. It is clear to point out that there are defences against a gun threat, but it would be clearly irresponsible to consider defences against attacks. You will also understand the law relating to the use of firearms.

# MULTIPLE ATTACKERS

### Introduction to multiple attackers

This element concentrates on multiple attackers. As previously mentioned the street gang cultures are becoming more prominent today and it is not just on the male side, women too go out at night in groups and with alcohol being readily available binge drinking now is not a gender biased subject. Without having awareness of this situation (not following the colour coding awareness system) you may at one time of your life fall prey to a multiple attacker situation.

### Multiple attacker defence

Unfortunately the movie industry casts the wrong impression of dealing with multiple attackers in that even though the good guy is surrounded by a number of attackers, he is only attacked one at a time whilst the others prepare themselves to move in. This couldn't be further from the truth and in fact, when confronted by a group of attackers, when one of the more dominant attackers initiate their attack the others wait until the victim is overwhelmed and then all at once join in, which makes this form of attack ferocious and potentially deadly.

Before we discuss the solutions to the problem it is best to reiterate the point of Awareness and Avoidance in that if you follow the Assumption that the potential attacker is not alone then you will be conscious of the third party.

### The Solution – Guiding Principles

If you are aware of multiple attacker scenarios and you are placed within one and you feel a true belief that you are in danger then consider a pre-emptive strike in order to disengage from the situation. The law is vague with this particular environment but if you believe you fear for your life and they have the Means, Opportunity and Intent to cause harm then use the pre-emptive strike to move into a better position or even better escape the situation. The five A's guiding principles you should adopt from the reactive stance are as follows:

**A  Avoid**

First thing you should do is obviously not be in the position in the first place and try to avoid any potential situation before you find yourself in one.

**A  Assume**

Always assume the attacker is in a group and not alone and that they are armed. If you do this it will aid your awareness.

**A  Awareness**

By assuming you should be aware of the relation and position they are to you and don't be afraid to use tactile sensitivity as this may give you an indication of where and by whom the attack will come from.

**A  Anticipate**

Anticipate any change of movement by the group and especially to your flanks, you should try to position yourself to either end of the group and not to be in the middle as you cannot control the situation.

**A  Action**

If you are past de-escalating the situation and you feel that you have lost control, then you need to consider the pre-emptive strike if the law is on your side and you have a true belief that it is going to get bad for you.

# WEAPONS AWARENESS

### Introduction to Weapons Awareness

On the streets of today, attackers are using weapons more and more and the severities of the attacks are becoming increasingly higher. The idea of this element is to bring you an awareness of weapons, the types and what they are capable of. Under the Prevention of Crime Act 1953 the law relating to weapons or an offensive weapon is defined as:

"ANY ARTICLE MADE OR ADAPTED FOR USE FOR CAUSING INJURY TO THE PERSON, OR INTENDED BY THE PERSON FOR SUCH USE".

The main understanding of the law should be focused on three words: Made, Adapted or Intended which we shall discuss in more detail later. There are three types of weapons: edged weapons (knives etc), hitting weapons (batons, truncheons, etc), or projectile weapons (firearms etc), all of which can be disguised or converted in some way to deceive their true intentions. During this module we will only be concerned with understanding and defence against edged weapons and an understanding of firearms attacks.

### Definition of edged weapons

The definition you need to understand, which has been taken in part from the Prevention of Crime Act 1953, is as follows:

"ANY ARTICLE MADE OR ADAPTED FOR USE FOR CAUSING INJURY TO THE PERSON, OR INTENDED BY THE PERSON FOR SUCH USE, WHICH WILL CUT, SLASH, LACERATE OR PUNCTURE THE BODY".

Unfortunately the movie industry casts the wrong impression of dealing with multiple attackers in that even though the good guy is surrounded by a number of attackers, he is only attacked one at a time whilst the others prepare themselves to move in.

### Types of edged weapons

**Made**

This item was made by a manufacturer, with the sole purpose to cause harm as a weapon to slash, cut, lacerate or puncture.

**Adapted**

This is an item that has been modified by a person which has the ability to cause harm from a slash, cut, lacerate or puncture.

**Intended**

This is an item that was designed and made for a purpose other than causing harm which is now intended to slash, cut, lacerate or puncture.

# EDGED WEAPONS DEFENCE

## Introduction to Edged Weapons Defence

As previously stated there are two types of situation you may find yourself within, which are being threatened with a knife with a goal to mug you or the full on attack, when the attacker is slashing and stabbing with the intent to cut you. Both of which are very serious and can lead to death. As previously mentioned within the detect manual:

**YOU ARE 56% MORE LIKELY TO BE MUGGED WITH A KNIFE THAN ANY OTHER WEAPON**

Edged weapons are so readily available to buy as there are so many knives made for purposes other than to cause harm, also, almost any implement can be made into an edged weapon to cause harm.

## The problem

There are many misconceptions with regards to attackers using knives or edged weapons, and that is their ability to use the weapon professionally. Most martial artists that teach weapons will have a moral, ethical and social respect for human life and to be honest if they were professionals you will most probably not see the knife at all. Another misconception is that attackers don't walk the streets with the knives out in the open and in their hands; they normally have them concealed, until they are ready to use them.

The two previously mentioned attacks with edged weapons are as follows:

## Threats

The knife or edged weapon normally is used in a fashion to show power and as such is shown to the victim and used around the headline (in a lot of cases). It is also accompanied by dialogue in that they will demand what they are after from you.

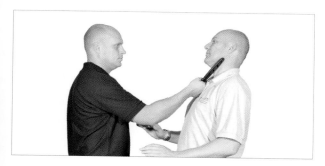

- Normally concealed at first.
- Used as a tool of force.
- Normally touching the body.
- Once they have what they want they may walk away.

## Attacks

When there has been a trigger to aggression and the attacker is using the weapon to slash, cut or stab you in order to inflict pain, damage or maim. The attack is normally ferocious and fast, which negates a lot of systems that train for the single stab..

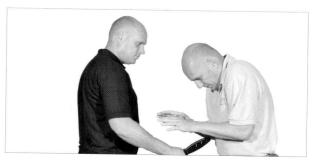

- Normally concealed at first.
- Used as a tool to inflict pain.
- Used at a distance.
- Not touching the body unless cutting you.
- Very fast erratic movements.
- Multi-directional.

## Threats Solution – guiding principles

Before the person threatens you, the knife or edged weapon will be concealed and the attack may start with some form of deception, such as a question like "excuse me, do you have the time?" to take your focus away from them getting the knife out. Once the knife has been drawn then it will be placed on you so that you are fully aware that it is a knife. Then the demand will be requested such as "give me your f***ing wallet or I'll cut you." At this stage the attacker has the Means, Opportunity and Intent to cause harm and as such you have the legal right to defend yourself. The following principles will minimise the lethal danger or the attack and provide you with a conceptual defence system.

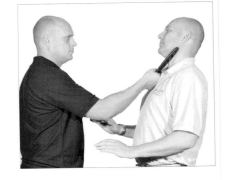

### Natural Guard
Made up of the flinch and survival mechanism where the hands will go to the knife or threat area automatically.

### Tactile Sensitivity
Create a non-obtrusive tactile sensitivity with the threat arm or hand that is natural with the flinch.

### Communicate
Communicate and confirm acceptance and compliance with the attacker. Then verbally distract the attacker.

### Pin
Rapidly pin the attacker's hand to yourself or to their medial part of their body.

### Attack
Due to the nature and severity of the attack then attack the vulnerable points.

## Attack Solution – guiding principles

For whatever reason an attacker uses an edged weapon or knife to attack you, the speed and ferocity of the attack is dependant on many factors such as environment, time of day or the anger and rage of the attacker. The main thing to note is that, you at this stage have no control over this. No matter what stab or slash the attacker throws, you must ensure you minimise the exposure of vulnerable parts of your body. Just by adopting the reactive stance will limit your vital areas up to 15% as opposed to the natural stance. Now some people say try to grab the knife hand to immobilise the attack, yes this is possible, however as soon as you have been cut which we agree will happen, you lose the ability to grab the arm as you will slide straight off due to blood. You should however treat the weapon arm as your target and attack the attack as it is presented to you. By doing this it is possible to feel the speed of the attack safely and immobilise their attacking arm to a point in which you are able to attack the vulnerable parts of the attacker's body. The following principles will provide you with a conceptual defence system.

### Active stance
Adopt this stance and keep tight and shoulders up covering the neck.

### Attack the Attack
Using both hands together strike the forearm of the attacker's knife arm, using palms or knuckles.

### Pain interrupt & vulnerable point
Once the attacker's speed has been interrupted by the pain they feel then strike the face or neck with both hands.

### Escape
As soon as you have interrupted the attack escape immediately (don't get into a clinch and wrestle over the weapon) as this is your primary directive.

# FIREARMS AWARENESS

### Introduction to Firearms Awareness

As you are aware it is an offence to carry a weapon in the eyes of the law, well in regards to firearms it is also an offence to buy, hold or own a firearm in the UK. We have categorised firearms as projectile weapons from how they are designed. Our definition of a firearm is as follows:

*"ANY ARTICLE OR MECHANISM MADE OR ADAPTED FOR USE FOR CAUSING INJURY TO THE PERSON, OR INTENDED BY THE PERSON FOR SUCH USE, WHICH WILL PROJECT A MISSILE UNDER FORCE".*

Like edged weapons defence you have two forms of an attack which are the attack and the threat, obviously an attack can be carried out from great distance dependant on the calibre and type of firearm, so the defence for this is almost down to the accuracy of the attacker.

One thing to point out here is that not all gunshot wounds will kill you, the reason why we mention this is that people who have been shot have died from the mere belief that all shooting wounds will kill, which has put them into shock and killed them.

### The Types

There are three main types of firearm (not including improvised ones) which are as follows:

### Revolvers

The revolver is a multi shot weapon that retains its cartridge in a revolving cylinder that works on a squeeze trigger mechanism and it is this cylinder that distinguishes the weapon from other hand guns.

### Semi & Automatic Pistols

The pistol can be semi automatic or automatic which means that as long as you have the required pressure on the trigger it will keep firing. Most of these handguns are gas and spring operated in that they eject the spent case and reload using the gas and the spring to operate.

### Semi & Automatic Rifles

The rifle is a long barrelled and higher calibre weapon which is or can be trigger or gas and spring operated. The range of a rifle is more significant than the pistol or revolver. In fact some rifles can fire over a mile.

- Limited amount of ammunition.
- The gas comes out from the cylinder as well as the barrel.
- The hammer strikes the percussion cap which fires the round.
- No empty case ejection.

- More ammunition can be fired.
- Can be automatic.
- Majority of gas comes from the barrel as it is reused to cock the weapon.
- The empty cartridge is ejected.
- Short ranges dependant on experience.

- Longer range.
- More ammunition.
- Fully automatic or single shot.
- Longer barrel.

# IMPROVISED WEAPONS AWARENESS

### Introduction to Improvised Weapons

When we say improvised weapon we are actually talking about disguised or covert weapons that are being hidden behind an ordinary item. Our definition is:

"ANY ARTICLE MADE OR ADAPTED TO DECEIVE AND CAMOUFLAGE THE TRUE IDENTITY WITH THE INTENT TO CAUSE INJURY OR HARM TO ANOTHER PERSON".

Some people carry them for personal security and protection others carry them with intent, it doesn't matter what the reason is as they are all illegal. So when someone has something in their hand don't dismiss it as being safe as you don't really know what it may be concealing. Information and photograph provided by Steve Collins PS5 Weapons Awareness.

---

## THINK POINT DEFEND 5

**5.1 PERFORM A PHYSICAL DEMONSTRATION OF THE DEFENCE AGAINST EDGED WEAPONS FOR:**
   A) A LONG RANGE ATTACK
   B) A MEDIUM RANGE ATTACK
   C) A CLOSE QUARTERS RANGE ATTACK
   D) A GROUND RANGE ATTACK

**5.2 PERFORM A PHYSICAL SCENARIO OF AN ATTACK TO DEVELOP MENTAL BLUEPRINTING.**

SEE YOUR INSTRUCTOR FOR WORKSHEET (IF YOU ARE TAKING EXAM)

# DESENSITIZE

# R.A.I.D Defence Cycle / Rapid Action Initiated Defence

1 Confidence    2 Awareness    3 Conflict Management    4 Defence    5 Aftermath

RATIONAL THOUGHT         EMOTIONAL THOUGHT

## DETER

Develop more confidence, through learning Specialist Skills, which will create a Non Victim mentality and provide you with a safer way of living.

## DETECT

Through Awareness and visual Observation skills, you will be able to foresee potential situations before they arise by subtle indicators or triggers.

## DEFUSE

By following our S.T.O.P conflict management process, you will be able to de-escalate the situation, whilst preparing the mind and body to Escape or Defend.

## DEFEND

RAID Defence, works on the body's natural reflexes, which combined with universal defence concepts, make it easy to learn and remember when you need it most.

## DESENSITIZE

After a violent confrontation, you may suffer from denial or mental stress. We will provide the tools, techniques and advice to enable your recovery process.

PRE-ASSAULT (PRO-ACTIVE)      ASSAULT (RE-ACTIVE)      POST-ASSAULT (ACTIVE)

© 2008 to H2H Defence & CTR Services Ltd

** This picture represents the processes of escalation from 1 to 5 of a physical confrontation unfolding

# WELCOME TO DESENSITIZE

**Founder/Chief Instructor**
Mr Tremaine Kent

Designed by Tremaine Kent, this is the final manual of the R.A.I.D. cycle. After a confrontation, whether mental or physical, will always be affected by the post traumatic effects such as denial or even legal or social consequence. During this module you will learn on the scene immediate first aid known as the self image drill (self triage), which helps you to get back your rational thought whilst checking your body for serious wounds. You will also learn reporting procedures so that you can remember what the attacker looked like to pass on to the police. You will also discover where to find help for coping with the post traumatic stress disorders (PTSD). This module is again overlooked but it is the only true way of learning from experience positively so that you may make a full recovery.

" **ONLY THROUGH ACCEPTANCE AND UNDERSTANDING – WILL YOU LEARN, DEVELOP AND MOVE FORWARD, WITH YOUR LIFE"**

# IMMEDIATE FIRST AID SELF IMAGE DRILL (SELF TRIAGE)

## Introduction

After a confrontation you will be feeling the psychological effects and more than likely be in an emotional state. As well as escaping the situation you need a directive to try and bring you back to a rational state quickly while you check your body for any injuries you may have incurred. The immediate first aid self image drill is a way in which you can systematically check all parts of the body for blood, pain or disfigurement, whilst bringing your rational thought back into use. There have been many documented cases, where individuals have been in a confrontation and not realised they have been stabbed until someone notices blood on their clothes. When they realise they have, they immediately go into shock due to elapsed time and loss of blood. When asked did they feel it, their response is "I thought I had just been punched." As previously mentioned your body will excrete a lot of endorphins into the body to cope with the physical confrontation which can mask the pain of such attacks.

## The Drill

The systematic check of the body starts with the most important areas first such as the head: use your palms and feel and lightly pat the areas of the head whilst constantly checking your palms for blood, then move down the body feeling the neck and shoulders, especially the armpits. Then the torso front and back, the arms and then the groin and backside and finally the legs:

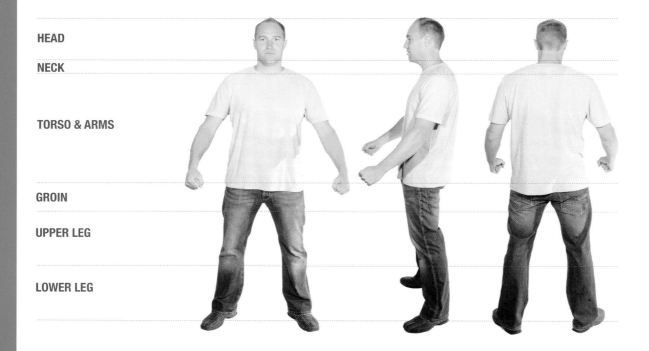

HEAD

NECK

TORSO & ARMS

GROIN

UPPER LEG

LOWER LEG

So let's say you have checked your head and upper torso and then you feel a damp patch on your back, check your hands for blood, if you are bleeding don't panic! You need to ascertain the seriousness of the wound and deal with it accordingly then keep checking the rest of the body; don't presume you only have one injury.

Whilst doing this drill you need to be conscious of finding an injury and what you are going to do if you are injured. Have some knowledge of first aid, so this drill can be completed on the move and preferably when walking or running towards a safe area or help. As previously mentioned if you have personal protection equipment such as SOS Protect

you should hit the panic button on your mobile and say as much as you can, this will alert the prescribed person and inform them if you have sustained injuries and your location.

## THINK POINT DESENSITIZE 1

**1.1 PERFORM A PHYSICAL DEMONSTRATION OF THE SELF IMAGE DRILL.**

SEE YOUR INSTRUCTOR FOR WORKSHEET (IF YOU ARE TAKING EXAM)

# REPORTING AN INCIDENT

### Introduction

After a confrontation, when you have escaped and you have checked yourself for injuries, you need to be able to recall as much information of the attacker so that you can give a good description to the authorities (police). This element will give you some ideas of how to remember what happened and what the attacker looked like by following the A to H attacker description code.

You also have to consider the mental trauma you may have sustained so you may not get all of these points. The A to H attacker description code is as follows:

**A Age**
The age of the attacker should be bracketed in years of five. So if you think the attacker is in his or her mid thirties then you should say from 30 to 35 years.

**B Build**
The build should be one of the following: slight, thin, athletic, medium, large, heavy or use other descriptive words that explain the build.

**C Clothes**
The clothes they wear should be described as colour on colour so if you had a male attacker wearing a black jacket with blue jeans then you would explain them as "black on blue". Also include the shoes.

**D Distinguishing Marks**
Such as tattoos, moles, scars or any other marks that stand out.

**E Elevation**
This relates to the height of the attacker and as most of you know your own height then take it from your own, where they are in relation to you.

**F Face**
The face should be explained by equating the look to someone famous and the shape of the head can be long, round etc, and also mention eye colour and the nose.

**G Gait**
This relates to how they walk and if they have any distinct abnormalities.

**H Hair**
What type and colour of hair they have and if they have facial hair such as a moustache or beard.

Don't forget that you should also try to remember any other relevant information such as weapons used and vehicles or mode of transport, and also the timings of the event. Any information you provide will aid the authorities in their investigations.

# WHERE TO FIND HELP

### Introduction

If you have been a victim of a physical attack or an assault, you may find it hard to talk to friends and family about your ordeal. The support they provide may place them in a position of denial, dependant on their relationship. So the need to talk to someone is important and there are many aid agencies or volunteer services available to you. If you go onto the internet and search for victim support you will find an abundance of information. Don't forget that H2H Defence staff are always here for you and we have had many victims talk to us regarding minimising the trauma and working on a recovery plan.

A lot of the volunteer services can provide professional counsellors that can talk to you about how you are feeling and reassure you that your feelings are normal and even healthy. With over millions of victims their experience has helped thousands of victims by listening, providing information, practical help and emotional support. The old saying of "a problem shared is a problem halved" comes into its own here and counsellors report that sharing the often strong feelings that follow a physical attack can help to reduce the length of time you will feel distressed.

### The proactive advice action

**People who are injured**

If you have been injured in a physical attack it is always best to get medical help. Sometimes you can be hurt more seriously than you realise, especially if you are suffering shock. If you can't work due to your injuries you should tell your employer. They may ask you to fill in a self-certification form or to get a sick note from your doctor or the hospital to show that you are unwell. You may be entitled to Statutory Sick Pay (SSP) if you are sick for four days or more. Your employer may pay you more than this depending on your contract of employment. You can get more information about benefits from the Benefits Agency or your local Citizens Advice Bureau (CAB).

Reporting the crime to the police: if you haven't informed the police already then it is up to you whether or not you report the crime to the police. It may help to talk this over with someone, such as a Victim Support volunteer first. If you want to claim Criminal Injuries Compensation you must report the attack to the police as soon as possible. Otherwise you can report the attack later, if you decide to. The police may take a statement from you and should tell you if someone has been arrested and cautioned or charged. Always tell the police if your attacker threatens or bothers you again, and even if you are just afraid that they might. When the police charge someone, they pass the evidence to the Crown Prosecution Service (CPS) who

then decide whether to take the case to court.

**Going to court**

If your case is taken to court by the Crown Prosecution Service (CPS), it may be several months before a date is set. Most cases are heard in the magistrates' court (which has three magistrates and no jury). Some more serious cases are heard in the Crown Court (which has a judge and jury). If the person charged with the offence pleads guilty, you may not be called to give evidence. But you should be told the date of the court case and you can attend the hearing, if you wish. If the person pleads not guilty, you will normally be asked to attend court to give evidence about what happened. The police will tell you if you need to appear in court as a witness. If this happens you don't have to go to court alone. You can usually take a friend or relative with you. Victim Support agencies run a Witness Service in every criminal court in England and Wales. The service gives support and information for victims and witnesses about what happens in court. The Witness Service can arrange visits to the court so that you can look around before the trial. They can also find you somewhere quiet to wait before and during the hearing, and they can help with other things such as expense claims forms.

## Compensation

As a victim of a physical attack you may be eligible for Criminal Injuries Compensation, but only if the crime was reported to the police as soon as practicably possible. The courts can order the person who attacked you to pay you compensation. The police should ask you about how the crime has affected you so that the court has the information to make a decision about this, alternatively, you may be able to take out a private prosecution or sue the person in a civil court to get compensation. You should get legal advice from a solicitor if you plan to do this. The costs involved in making a claim will vary. Find out how much you might have to pay before entering into any agreement.

The best way of getting help is to speak to your H2H Defence Instructor and they will advise you on where to find advice and help. Alternatively if you look on the internet there is an abundance of related victim services and sites.

## THINK POINT DESENSITIZE 2

**2.1. ANALYSE WHAT SUPPORT GROUPS ARE AVAILABLE TO AID IN RECOVERY AFTER A CONFRONTATION OR AN ATTACK.**

SEE YOUR INSTRUCTOR FOR WORKSHEET (IF YOU ARE TAKING EXAM)

# TRAINING

### Introduction

After a physical attack, when the incident has been dealt with by the police and possibly the court system, H2H Defence believes, through previous students' experiences, training can aid in the recovery process as it creates a mindset of coping, sharing and rebuilding the survival mindset. Your instructor can arrange one on one sessions to help you regain your confidence over time.

The saying "a healthy body gives you a healthy mind" is never a truer word spoken and by taking up some form of physical exercise, whether it is walking, jogging, gym or following martial arts, you will be able to rebuild the psychological void an attack can create.

The types of training you can undertake, which will help your recovery, are as follows:

### Fitness Training

There are many benefits of fitness training from developing your cardiovascular, aerobic, strength, endurance and skill, but the biggest benefit of all is your wellbeing due to the fact that when you do any exercise the body excretes endorphins and you feel somewhat better physically and emotionally. This benefit helps you mentally in that you will be able to cope with stress more as your body is fitter. If you are new to fitness training then you should start slow and preferably seek the approval of your doctor and have a professional create an achievable training program.

### Martial Arts Training

The training you do with H2H Defence is self defence training and it can be enhanced further if you study some form of martial arts on a regular basis. Martial art training provides discipline, etiquette, and sport orientated competitive edge. By completing regular classes you will develop your basic combat arts and tool development; this also promotes fitness due to stretching, repetition and sparing. You should look at local martial arts classes near you and speak to your H2H Defence instructor about what discipline would be good for you.

## Self Defence Training

H2H Defence was specifically designed to follow a conflict from start to finish and in particular pre and post assault phases. We generally find that students take self defence classes to gain confidence and awareness rather than the typical physical defence methodologies or techniques provided by many. By attending regular classes you will develop the personal security awareness training needed for the streets of today and also conflict management which seems to be the crucial link between a potential of a physical attack and a full blown attack. A lot of martial arts instructors try to combine their teachings with self defence which has been found in some cases to be ineffective, due to the law and legislation and the fact that there are no rules on the street. As soon as you start learning to attack an attacker then you have to consider the consequence of your actions and the law surrounding those actions, covered in previous manuals. The common saying by many instructors, "it's better to be judged by three than carried by six" is ok if your life is in impending danger. However you can't rely on this all the time and it tends to be used with the lack of knowledge and understanding. If you are serious about your own personal security you will attend regular classes to learn how to build personal defence into your life and not just an hour a week.

You should be able to create a safe living and working environment through procedures and knowledge that is achievable and not security overwhelming. This environment should minimise your exposure to potential physical confrontations or attacks.

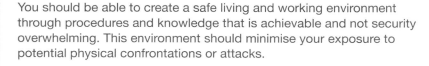

## THINK POINT DESENSITIZE 3

**3.1. EXPLAIN HOW TRAINING CAN HELP WITH RECOVERY AFTER A CONFRONTATION OR AN ATTACK.**

SEE YOUR INSTRUCTOR FOR WORKSHEET (IF YOU ARE TAKING EXAM)

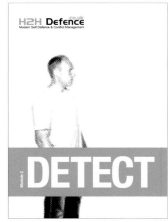

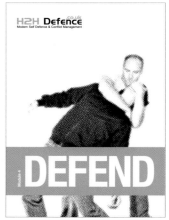